SOCCER MADE EASY™

PRESENTS

The World Youth Training Program
Coaching 13 - 16 Year Olds

by Shaun Green

REEDSWAIN

**Library of Congress
Cataloging - in - Publication Data**

by Shaun Green
    The World Youth Training Program
    Coaching 13-16 Year Olds

ISBN No. 1-59164-038-5
Lib. of Congress Catalog No. 2002094140
© 2002

Editing
Bryan R. Beaver

Cover Photos by
Robyn McNeil

Printed by
DATA REPRODUCTIONS
Auburn, Michigan

Reedswain Publishing
612 Pughtown Road
Spring City, PA 19475
800.331.5191
www.reedswain.com
info@reedswain.com

Contents

Chapter 3
Coaching Methodology........................... 117

Chapter 4
Team Management.............................. 147

Chapter 5
Equipment... 163

Acknowledgements

There are several people I would like to thank for their help with the production of this book.

First my wife Laurie and sons Kenny, Shane and Adam. Without their support and encouragement it would not have been possible. To Stan Nixon and Peter Kirkley, my former youth coaches, for being great role models and inspiring me to make coaching my career.

To my numerous friends in coaching who have shared their ideas and provided input.

Last but not least, all the players I have been fortunate to coach. I have learned from each one of them and feel privileged to have had them in my life.

Introduction

This book has been specifically designed to provide youth clubs and coaches with a progressive and comprehensive coaching curriculum for players ages 13 to 16 years. The content is age appropriate with an emphasis on skill development while having fun.

Each practice uses drills and games performed by top coaches world-wide. The content lays out the entire season, step by step, in an easy to understand format.

In addition to practice sessions for the entire season for each age group, all the important skills in Passing, Ball Control, Shooting, Heading, Dribbling, Defending and Goalkeeping are explained. Additional sections feature Coaching Methodology, Team Management, Safety and Equipment.

Chapter 1

A Twelve-Week Training Program for
Ages 13 through 16 years

This section provides you with a Twelve-Week Training Program for players ages 13 through 16 years. Each practice features four fun and progressive drills and culminates with a small-sided game.

Emphasis is placed on the continued development of fundamental skills and careful consideration has been given to prioritize the most relevant techniques to master at this age level.

Passing and ball control are the main theme of the training program with additional practices for shooting, dribbling and heading. There is a great emphasis on the introduction of Aerial Passing and Control, Small group concepts and Pressurized games and drills.

The program is age appropriate and sets a solid foundation for players to advance to the next level. Each practice uses drills performed by top coaches worldwide. The program is meant as a guideline and coaches are encouraged to incorporate a minimal understanding of team tactics and laws of the game.

Weekly Practice Schedule

Week One — Ages 13 to 16 Years

Technique	Practice	Emphasis
Passing	Hit the Ball	Pace, Accuracy
Passing	One Touch, Two Touch	Decision Making, Pace, Accuracy
Passing	Pressure Passing II	Mechanics - Intense Repetitions
Passing	Passing Rotary	Mechanics - Intense Repetitions
Theme reinforced in small-sided game (with goalkeepers)		

Week Two — Ages 13 to 16 Years

Technique	Practice	Emphasis
Passing	Mechanics of The Chip Pass	Pure Mechanics - Static
Passing	Mechanics of The Bent Pass	Pure Mechanics - Static
Passing	Mechanics of The Lofted Pass	Pure Mechanics - Static
Passing	Aerial Passing Drill	
Theme reinforced in small-sided game (with goalkeepers)		

Week Three — Ages 13 to 16 Years

Technique	Practice	Emphasis
Passing	Return the Pass	Pace, Accuracy, Movement
Passing	Pass and Overlap	Pace, Accuracy, Timing
Passing	First Man, Second Man	Pace, Accuracy, Movement
Passing	8 v 2 Keep Away	Disguise, Pace, Accuracy, Timing
Theme reinforced in small-sided game (with goalkeepers)		

Week Four — Ages 13 to 16 Years

Technique	Practice	Emphasis
Passing	The Color Game	Vision, Decision Making
Passing	Sit on the Ball	Creating Space
Passing	Through the Gate	Short Range Passing
Passing	Pressure Passing	Pace, Accuracy, Movement
Theme reinforced in small-sided game (with goalkeepers)		

Week Five — Ages 13 to 16 Years

Technique	Practice	Emphasis
Passing	Passing and Support	Movement off the ball
Passing	Pass outside the Grid	Pace, Accuracy, Timing, Movement
Passing	3 v 1 Passing under pressure	Pace, Accuracy, Timing, Movement
Passing	3 v 1 Swap Over	Pace, Accuracy, Timing, Movement

Theme reinforced in small-sided game (with goalkeepers)

Week Six — Ages 13 to 16 Years

Technique	Practice	Emphasis
Passing	2 v 2 Passing under pressure	Disguise, Pace, Timing , Accuracy
Passing	4 v 2 Both Sides	Disguise, Pace, Timing , Accuracy
Passing	4 v 4 Passing under pressure	Forward Passing, Penetration
Passing	4 v 4 Play from the back	Forward Passing, Penetration

Theme reinforced in small-sided game (with goalkeepers)

Week Seven — Ages 13 to 16 Years

Technique	Practice	Emphasis
Ball Control	Getting behind the ball	Anticipation
Ball Control	Pass and Receive	Control, Turn, Preparation
Ball Control	Wedge Control Relay	Mechanics - Jog/Game Speed
Ball Control	Wedge Control in Pairs	Mechanics under pressure

Theme reinforced in small-sided game (with goalkeepers)

Week Eight — Ages 13 to 16 Years

Technique	Practice	Emphasis
Ball Control	Control and Turn	Close Control while Turning
Ball Control	Wedge Control Relay and Turn	Close Control while Turning
Ball Control	Rotary Thigh Control	Mechanics - Intense Repetitions
Ball Control	Rotary Chest Control	Mechanics - Intense Repetitions

Theme reinforced in small-sided game (with goalkeepers)

Week Nine — Ages 13 to 16 Years

Technique	Practice	Emphasis
Shooting	2 v 1 Running Goalkeeper	Variety of Shooting techniques
Shooting	Shooting Center and Wide	Long and Short range Shooting
Shooting	Give and Go Edge of the Box	Timing of Runs - Technique
Shooting	Shooting World Cup Drill	Technique - Repetitions

Theme reinforced in small-sided game (with goalkeepers)

Week Ten — Ages 13 to 16 Years

Technique	Practice	Emphasis
Heading	Heading for Distance	Mechanics, Power, Accuracy
Heading	Heading Midfield Battles	Defensive and Offensive techniques
Heading	World Cup Heading 2 v 2	Accuracy and Power
Heading	World Cup Heading at Goal	Technique - Repetitions

Theme reinforced in small-sided game (with goalkeepers)

Week Eleven — Ages 13 to 16 Years

Technique	Practice	Emphasis
Defending	Defending 1 v1	Mechanics, Timing, Attitude
Defending	Defending 1 v 2	Mechanics, Timing, Decision Making
Defending	Defending 1 v 1 Swap Grid	Mechanics, Timing, Decision Making
Defending	Defending 1 v1 around the Box	Positioning, Timing, Technique

Theme reinforced in small-sided game (with goalkeepers)

Week Twelve — Ages 13 to 16 Years

Technique	Practice	Emphasis
Dribbling	Explosive Body Movement	Body Feints. Fakes, Moves
Dribbling	Slalom through cones	Control when running with ball
Dribbling	Dribble, Turn, Escape	Change of Speed/direction
Dribbling	Dribbling 1 v 1	Change of Speed/ Direction

Theme reinforced in small-sided game (with goalkeepers)

Hit the Ball

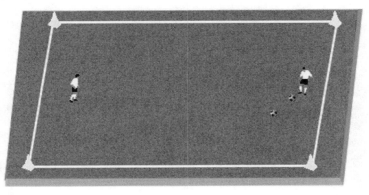

Objective:
This practice is designed to improve the correct mechanics involved in the execution of the "Push Pass", with an emphasis on accuracy.

Instructions:
Two players are positioned in a grid 20 yards x 20 yards. One player starts the practice with two balls. The player passes the first ball to his partner to control and redirect approximately 2 to 5 yards in front of him. He then passes the second ball for his partner to redirect and try to hit the first ball.

The coach should emphasize the following coaching points:

- Keep the feet moving and be balanced at all times.
- Develop a feel for the correct distance you need to redirect the ball.
- Adjust the body position to hit the ball with the pass.
- Give firm and accurate passes to your partner's feet when serving.

The first player to hit the ball 3 times wins. Rotate so different players compete against each other.

Equipment:
Grid 20 yards by 20 yards
2 Players
2 Balls
4 Cones

One touch, Two touch

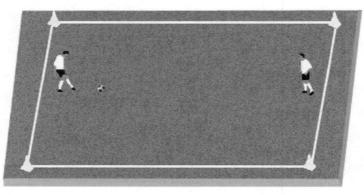

Objective:

This practice is designed to improve a player's quick thinking to play one or two touch passes.

Instructions:

Two players are positioned in a grid 10 yards x 10 yards. The practice starts when one player passes the ball to his partner. At the same time he passes the ball he must shout out either "one" or "two". When receiving the ball his partner must take as many touches as the number called. If the number is "one" he must pass the ball back first time. If the number is "two" he must control the ball on the first touch and return the pass on the second touch. When returning the pass to his partner he also calls out a number.

Players are awarded a point for every mistake their partner makes.
First player to get five points wins.
Rotate so different players compete against each other.

The coach should emphasize the following coaching points:

- Make sure players call out the number at the same time they pass the ball to allow time for the receiving player to react.
- Players should always be alert and light on their feet.
- Deliver quality accurate ground passes.
- If the player has to take a touch before passing, ensure that the first touch is played in front and out of his feet, enabling him to easily pass the ball on his second touch.

Equipment:
Grid 10 yards by 10 yards,
2 Players,
1 Ball,
4 Cones

6

Pressure Passing

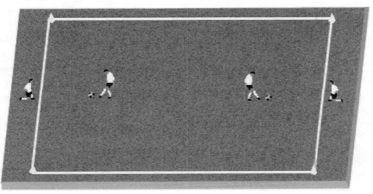

Objective:

This practice is designed to improve the technical ability of the "Push Pass" with an emphasis on "pace and accuracy".

Instructions:

Place a server with a ball at both sides of the grid. Each server passes the ball to the two receivers to pass back "first time". The players in the center should work at full speed and concentrate on quality first touch passing.

If a working player turns to a server for a pass, and the server is retrieving the ball, the player must continue to run and turn to receive the ball from the opposite server. The player should not wait for a server to retrieve the ball.

Competitions should be played e.g.: how many passes in 60 seconds, the first player to reach 20 good passes. Only passes made on the ground are countable.

Equipment:

Grid 10 yards by 10 yards
4 Players
2 Balls
4 Cones

Passing Rotary

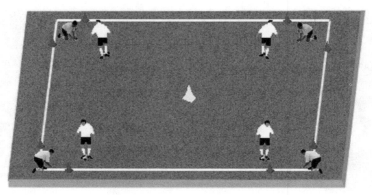

Objective:

This practice is designed to improve the technical ability of the "Push Pass" with an emphasis on "pace and accuracy".

Instructions:

A server is positioned at each corner of the grid. The grid is approximately 20 yards x 20 yards. Each server has a ball. Four players are positioned inside the grid, each player opposite a server. The server rolls a ball through the two cones for the receiver to pass back first time using the push pass. The player must pass the ball back through the cones and on the ground to receive a point. After passing the ball, the player must check to the center cone and rotate to the right and receive a pass from the next server. Each player works to see how many good passes he can make in 30 seconds. After the 30-second period is completed, the coach compares scores, and the servers switch with the receivers.

Equipment:

Grid 20 yards by 20 yards
8 Players
4 Balls
9 Cones

Small-Sided Game

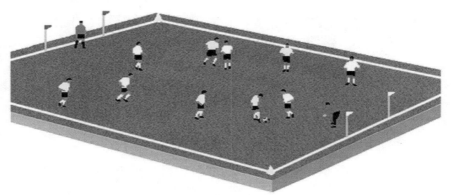

Finish with small sided game with goalkeepers.

Instructions:

The practice should be concluded with a small-sided game reinforcing the coaching points from your drills.

- Divide the players into two equal teams with goalkeepers.
- Each field should be approximately 40 yards x 60 yards.
- Use corner flags or cones as goals.
- Total time, 30 minutes.

At the end of your session, review all coaching points made during the practice.

Team 1 score _____ v Team 2 score _____

IMPORTANT ANNOUNCEMENTS FOR NEXT GAME/PRACTICE:

Mechanics of the Chip Pass

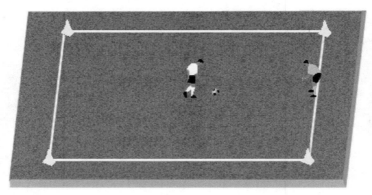

Objective:
This practice is designed to improve the technical ability of the "Chip Pass" with an emphasis on accuracy.

Instructions:
Two players are positioned within the grid, one serving, and one receiving. The server rolls the ball for the player to chip back to hands. The object is for the player chipping the ball to gradually move further away from the server and maintain the accuracy of the chip pass. The player should increase the distance in five-yard increments, moving only when a successful chip pass is made into the hands of the server.

Equipment:
Grid 20 yards by 10 yards
2 Players, 1 Ball, 4 Cones

Mechanics of the Bent Pass

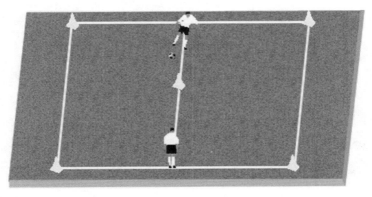

Objective:
This practice is designed to introduce players to the correct mechanics involved in the execution of the "Bent Pass".

Instructions:
Two players are positioned at opposite sides of the grid. A cone is placed directly in-between players. Players alternate passing the ball around the cone using the "Bent Pass".

Equipment:
Grid 10 yards by 10 yards
2 Players
1 Ball, 5 Cones

Mechanics of the Lofted Pass

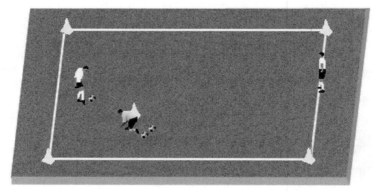

Objective:

This practice is designed to introduce the correct mechanics involved in the execution of the "Lofted Pass".

Instructions:

Three players are positioned in a grid 20 yards x 10 yards. One player acts as a server, one as a receiving player and the other to catch the lofted pass. The server rolls the ball for the receiver to pass first time to the catcher at the opposite end of the grid. Rotate regularly to provide each player an opportunity to act as the receiver.

Equipment:

Grid 20 yards by 10 yards
3 Players, 1 Ball, 5 Cones

Aerial Passing Drill

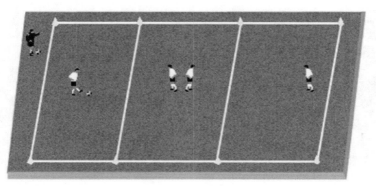

Objective:

This practice is designed to introduce players to the correct mechanics involved in the execution of the "Bent, Lofted and Chip Pass."

Instructions:

Four players are positioned within the grid, two serving, and two receiving. The server passes the ball for the player to pass around the server to the receiver at the opposite end of the grid.

The receiver controls the ball, passes to the server and the practice is repeated from that side. Players are restricted to using aerial passes only.

Rotate the servers with the receivers every five minutes.

Equipment:

Grid 30 yards by 20 yards
4 Players
1 Ball
8 Cones

Small-Sided Game

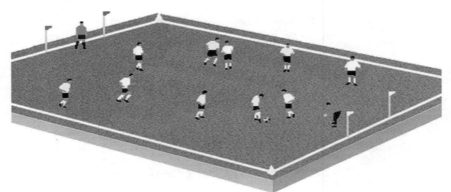

Finish with small sided game with goalkeepers.

Instructions:

The practice should be concluded with a small-sided game reinforcing the coaching points from your drills.

- Divide the players into two equal teams with goalkeepers.
- Each field should be approximately 40 yards x 60 yards.
- Use corner flags or cones as goals.
- Total time, 30 minutes.

At the end of your session, review all coaching points made during the practice.

Team 1 score _____ v Team 2 score _____

IMPORTANT ANNOUNCEMENTS FOR NEXT GAME/PRACTICE:

Return the Pass

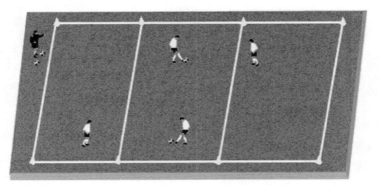

Objective:

This practice is designed to improve the technical ability of the "Push Pass" with emphasis on "pace and accuracy".

Instructions:

Two pairs of players are positioned in opposite grids. Players start the practice by passing the ball quickly around their own grid. On the coach's command the player in possession of the ball runs directly to the free player in the opposite grid and makes a pass, receives the return pass, then runs back to his own grid and repeats the practice.

Equipment:

Grid 30 yards by 10 yards
4 Players
2 Balls
8 Cones

15

Pass and Overlap

Objective:

This practice is designed to improve the technical ability of the "Push Pass" with an emphasis on the "over-lapping run".

Instructions:

Two pairs of players are positioned in opposite grids. Players start the practice by passing the ball quickly around their own grid. On the coach's command the players exchange grids using an overlapping run. Once both pairs of players are in the opposite grid the practice is repeated.

Equipment:

Grid 30 yards by 10 yards
4 Players
2 Balls
8 Cones

First Man, Second Man

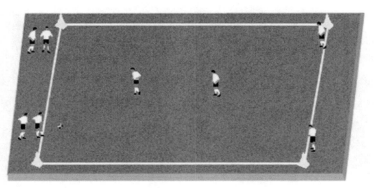

Objective:
This practice is designed to improve each player's technical ability in short range passing with an emphasis on "pace and accuracy".

Instructions:
- An area is marked out approximately 20 yards by 20 yards.
- Two receivers are placed 5 yards apart in the center of the grid.
- Four players are positioned at one end of the grid and two at the opposite end.

The practice starts with the first player passing the ball to the nearest receiver. The receiver then passes to the first player in the second group. After receiving the ball, the player passes to the second receiver, who passes to the runner. Both players run to the opposite end and the practice is repeated from the opposite side.

Equipment:
Grid 20 yards by 20 yards
8 Players
1 Ball
4 Cones

8 v 2 Keep Away

Objective:
This practice is designed to improve each player's technical ability in short range passing with an emphasis on "disguise, pace, accuracy and timing".

Instructions:
- An area is marked out approximately 20 yards by 20 yards.
- A group of players are positioned around the outside of the grid.
- Two defenders are placed in the center of the grid and wear different colored vests.

The object of this practice is for the players on the outside of the grid to maintain possession of the ball by using one or two touch passes. Whenever possible the players must try to pass in between the two defenders. A goal is awarded for ten consecutive passes and each time the defenders are split with a pass. The player responsible for losing possession swaps with one of the defenders.

Equipment:
Grid 20 yards by 20 yards
Group of players
1 Ball
4 Cones

Small-Sided Game

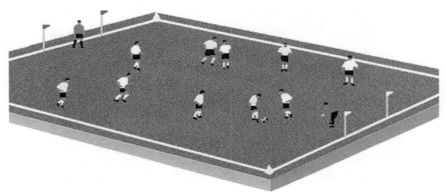

Finish with small sided game with goalkeepers.

Instructions:

The practice should be concluded with a small-sided game reinforcing the coaching points from your drills.

- Divide the players into two equal teams with goalkeepers.
- Each field should be approximately 40 yards x 60 yards.
- Use corner flags or cones as goals.
- Total time, 30 minutes.

At the end of your session, review all coaching points made during the practice.

Team 1 score _____ v Team 2 score _____

IMPORTANT ANNOUNCEMENTS FOR NEXT GAME/PRACTICE:

The Color Game

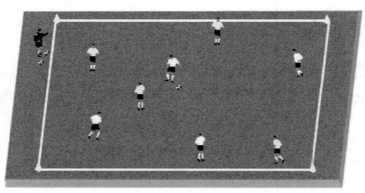

Objective:
This practice is designed to improve each player's vision when passing the ball.

Instructions:
An area is marked out approximately 30 yards by 30 yards. Divide players into two groups and identify each team with different colored vests. Players move around the grid passing the ball "two touch". The passes must always be in the sequence of "Red Player - Yellow Player" (red can only pass to yellow and yellow to red). This forces players to scan the area before receiving the pass. Progress to "one touch" play. Encourage players on the ball to pass over a variety of distances, not always a short pass. Encourage players off the ball to get into a position in line with the player's vision (don't hide). Condition the players "not to talk or clap" for the ball.
All communication is visual. Then remove condition.

Progression:
On the coach's command the player in possession must pass to the player named by the coach. When the coach shouts "Johnny", the player in possession must quickly scan the field, locate Johnny, and pass quickly to his feet. The play is continued with the "Red-Yellow" sequence until the coach calls another name.

Equipment:
Grid 30 yards by 30 yards
Group of players
1 Ball
4 Cones

Sit on the Ball

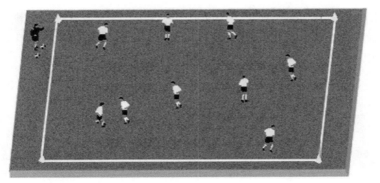

Objective:
This practice is designed to help players create space when passing as a group.

Instructions:
- An area is marked out approximately 30 yards by 30 yards.
- Small Group, plus one defender are positioned within the grid.

The players must attempt to keep possession from the defender within the grid. The team scores a goal each time a player can receive the ball in enough space to "sit on the ball".

The supporting players must always work to offer the deepest and widest possible angles for the player in possession. The supporting players should ask themselves two questions when supporting the player in possession:

- How wide can I get to give the best possible passing lane?
- How far from the player can I get to give the maximum time on the ball when the pass is received?

Rotate working defender frequently to ensure high pressure.

Equipment:
Grid 30 yards by 30 yards
Small group of players
1 Ball
4 Cones

Through the Gate

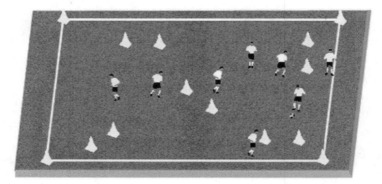

Objective:

This practice is designed to encourage quality short range passing and good support off the ball.

Instructions:

- An area is marked out approximately 40 yards by 40 yards.
- A Small group and two defenders are positioned within the grid.
- Gates 1 yard apart are set up throughout the grid.

The object of this practice is for the group of players to keep possession of the ball and try to pass the ball through any of the gates. A goal is awarded for each pass through the gate. Players must be in a position to receive the ball through the gate. Passes made into space through the gate do not count. Players cannot score consecutively through the same gate. Players in possession are awarded one goal for 10 consecutive passes.

Defenders must try to prevent the players from passing the ball through the gates. Rotate players so each player performs the role of the defender.

Equipment:

Grid 40 yards by 40 yards
Group of players
1 Ball
Supply of cones

22

Pressure Passing

Objective:

This practice is designed to improve the technical ability of the "Push Pass" with an emphasis on accuracy and explosive movement off the ball.

Instructions:

Two players are positioned in the grid with the remainder of the group spread evenly around the outside of the grid. A minimum of 10 balls is scattered inside the grid. On the coach's command, the two players within the grid have 2 minutes to make as many passes as they can to the outside players. After receiving a pass, the servers pass the ball back into an open area in the grid.

Players must work at full speed and concentrate on quality passing. Outside players should be constantly talking and alert for passes. Rotate two middle players every two minutes.

Equipment:

Grid 20 yards by 20 yards
Group of players
Supply of balls
4 Cones

Small-Sided Game

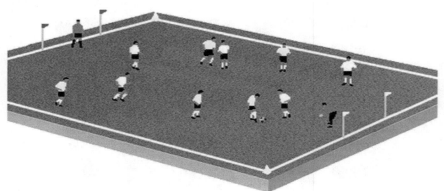

Finish with small sided game with goalkeepers.

Instructions:

The practice should be concluded with a small-sided game reinforcing the coaching points from your drills.

- Divide the players into two equal teams with goalkeepers.
- Each field should be approximately 40 yards x 60 yards.
- Use corner flags or cones as goals.
- Total time, 30 minutes.

At the end of your session, review all coaching points made during the practice.

Team 1 score _____ v Team 2 score _____

IMPORTANT ANNOUNCEMENTS FOR NEXT GAME/PRACTICE:

Passing and Support

Objective:

This practice is designed to improve short range passing with an emphasis on quality movement off the ball.

Instructions:

Four players are positioned on the outside lines of a grid 10 yards by 10 yards. Players pass the ball around the outside of the grid. After passing the ball the player should offer a good supporting angle. Players should be constantly moving their feet and asking for the ball. Care should be taken on the speed of the pass and the pass should be accurate to the player's feet.

Equipment:

Grid 10 yards by 10 yards
4 Players
1 Ball
4 Cones

Pass outside the Grid

Objective:
This practice is designed to improve the technical ability of the "Push Pass" with an emphasis on "pace, accuracy and timing".

Instructions:
- A grid is marked off 10 yards by 10 yards.
- A player is positioned on each side of the grid.
- One defender is placed in the center of the grid.
- Two resting defenders are stationed outside the grid.

The object of the practice is for the four players on the outside of the grid to keep possession of the ball without it being intercepted by the center defender. The outside players cannot enter the grid and the pressurizing defender cannot leave the grid. The outside players receive a goal for eight consecutive passes. Increase the number of passes per goal to challenge players.
Coach can also place a condition of one or two touch passing.

Rotate working defender with resting defender frequently to ensure high pressure. Rotate players so each player performs the role of the defender.

The coach should emphasize the following coaching points:

- Players should always be alert and light on their feet.
- Disguise your intentions before passing the ball by using head fakes and body feints.
- Deliver quality accurate ground passes to feet.
- Deliver a pass your partner can hit first time.
- Consider the speed of the pass, not too hard and not too soft.
- Offer a good supporting angle once you have passed the ball.
- Communicate with the player in possession of ball.

Equipment:
Grid 10 yards by 10 yards, 6 Players, 1 Ball, 4 Cones

3 v 1 Passing under pressure

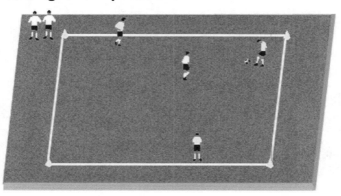

Objective:

This practice is designed to improve the technical ability of the "Push Pass" with an emphasis on "disguise, pace, accuracy and timing".

Instructions:

Three players are positioned within a grid 10 yards by 10 yards. The three players must try to keep possession from the defender. The three players in possession may move anywhere within the grid. The defender's goal is to dispossess the players in possession.

The two supporting players must always work to offer the deepest and widest possible angles for the player in possession. The supporting players should ask themselves two questions when supporting the player in possession:

- How wide can I get to give the best possible passing lane?
- How far from the player can I get to give the maximum time on the ball when the pass is received?

The player in possession must look to disguise his passing intentions by using step-overs, body feints and head fakes. He must also have the discipline to hold on to the ball and commit the defender towards him. If he releases the ball too early the defender will have less ground to cover to put pressure on the receiving player.

Players in possession are awarded one goal for 10 consecutive passes. Rotate working defender with resting defender frequently to ensure high pressure. Rotate players so each player performs the role of the defender.

Equipment:
Grid 10 yards by 10 yards
6 Players,
1 Ball,
4 Cones

3 v 1 Swap Over

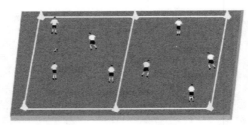

Objective:
This practice is designed to improve each player's technical ability in short range passing with an emphasis on "disguise, pace, accuracy and timing".

Instructions:
- An area is marked out approximately 20 yards by 20 yards.
- The grid is divided into two grids of 10 yards by 10 yards.
- Four players are positioned in each grid.
- Teams wear different colored vests.
- Players are numbered one through four on each team.

The practice starts with both groups of four players keeping possession playing one and two touch passes. The coach calls out a number one through four. When the player's number is called, that player immediately runs to the opposite grid creating a 3 v1 situation and tries to win the ball. The first team to win the ball is awarded a goal. The defenders then return the their own grid and the practice is repeated with a different player defending.

The supporting players must always work to offer the deepest and widest possible angles for the player in possession. The supporting players should ask themselves two questions when supporting the player in possession:

- How wide can I get to give the best possible passing lane?
- How far from the player can I get to give the maximum time on the ball when the pass is received?

The player in possession must look to disguise his passing intentions using step-overs, body feints and head fakes. He must also have the discipline to hold on to the ball and commit the defender towards him.
If he releases the ball too early the defender will have less ground to cover to put pressure on the receiving player.

Equipment:
Grid 20 yards by 20 yards,
8 Players,
2 Balls,

28

Small-Sided Game

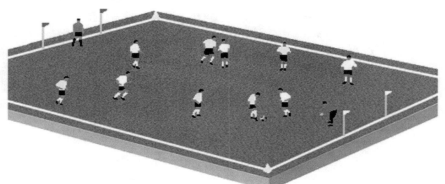

Finish with small sided game with goalkeepers.

Instructions:

The practice should be concluded with a small-sided game reinforcing the coaching points from your drills.

- Divide the players into two equal teams with goalkeepers.
- Each field should be approximately 40 yards x 60 yards.
- Use corner flags or cones as goals.
- Total time, 30 minutes.

At the end of your session, review all coaching points made during the practice.

Team 1 score _____ v Team 2 score _____

IMPORTANT ANNOUNCEMENTS FOR NEXT GAME/PRACTICE:

2 v 2 Passing under pressure

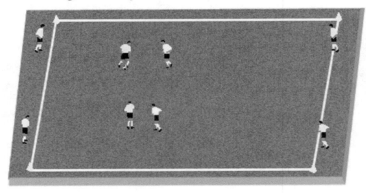

Objective:

This practice is designed to improve the tactical understanding of the 2 v 2 situation with an emphasis on "disguise, pace, accuracy and timing".

Instructions:

Eight players are positioned in a grid 30 yards x 20 yards. A player is positioned at each corner of the grid. Four players are positioned inside the grid, in teams of two. The practice starts with a ball played from one of the end players to either of the pairs in the grid. Whichever pair wins the ball must try to turn and play a pass to the players at the opposite end of the grid. If the same pair are successful they then receive the ball back from the end player and try to repeat the practice to the opposite end of the grid.

The two players not in possession must try to win the ball and find one of the corner players with a pass. A goal is scored for each successful pass. A goal cannot be scored in succession from the same side. Back passes can be made.

Players in the center should work for approximately 5 minutes then rotate with players in the corners. The four players in the corners of the grid should constantly be looking for passes from the central players. When passing a ball to a central player he should tell the player to "hold the ball, turn, man-on or play the ball back".

Equipment:

Grid 30 yards by 20 yards
8 Players
1 Ball, 4 Cones

4 v 2 Both Sides

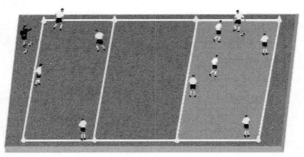

Objective:
This practice is designed to improve each player's technical ability in short range passing with an emphasis on "disguise, pace, accuracy and timing".

Instructions:
- An area is marked out approximately 20 yards by 30 yards.
- Three inner grids are marked 10 yards long and 20 yards wide.
- Four players are positioned in each of the end grids.
- Two defenders are placed in the center grid. Defenders must wear different colored vests.

The practice starts with one group of four players keeping possession from the two defenders. The four players must obtain a minimum of four consecutive passes then pass the ball to the opposite team. The two defenders must try to win the ball. Rotate players so each player performs the role of the defender.

The supporting players must always work to offer the deepest and widest possible angles for the player in possession. The supporting players should ask themselves two questions when supporting the player in possession:

- How wide can I get to give the best possible passing lane?
- How far from the player can I get to give the maximum time on the ball when the pass is received?

The player in possession must look to disguise his passing intentions using step-overs, body feints and head fakes. He must also have the discipline to hold on to the ball and commit the defender towards him. If he releases the ball too early the defender will have less ground to cover to put pressure on the receiving player.

Equipment:
Grid 20 yards by 30 yards,
10 Players,
1 Ball,
8 Cones

4 v 4 Passing under pressure

Objective:
This practice is designed to improve "forward" passing.

Instructions:
Use two teams of six players. Four players in each team are positioned and restricted to the center grid. Two players on each team act as "target players" and are placed in the end grid on the same side as their team.

The coach begins the practice by serving a lofted ball into the center grid. Both teams fight for possession. Once a team has possession the object is to play the ball forward to one of the two "target players" as quickly as possible using the minimum amount of passes. A goal is scored by successfully passing the ball to the target player's feet.

Players should use various techniques such as dribbling, turning, crossover runs and the "wall pass" to position themselves for forward passes.

The coach should keep the service rapid and serve the next ball as soon as a goal is scored.
Rotate target players with two central players every five minutes.

Equipment:
Grid 40 yards by 20 yards
12 Players
Supply of Balls
8 Cones

4 v 4 Play from the Back

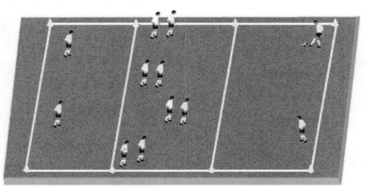

Objective:
This practice is designed to improve "forward" passing.

Instructions:
Eight players are positioned within the center grid. The four players are marked by four defending players and restricted to the center grid. The attacking team has two supporting defenders and two target players, both restricted to their respective grids.

The practice begins from the defensive zone. The two defensive players must play the ball to an attacking player and support the ball. The defensive players may interact with each other and pass the ball back and forth when they have possession.

Once the attacking midfielders have possession the object is to play the ball forward to one of the two "target players" as quickly as possible using the minimum amount of passes. Defensive players must try to win the ball.

Players should use various techniques such as dribbling, turning, crossover runs and the "wall pass" to position themselves for forward passes

A goal is scored by successfully passing the ball to the target player's feet. Once the target receives a pass, he now becomes the defensive player and starts play from that side. Rotate center players with supporting players at the appropriate time.

Equipment:
Grid 30 yards by 20 yards
12 Players
1 Ball, 8 Cones

Small-Sided Game

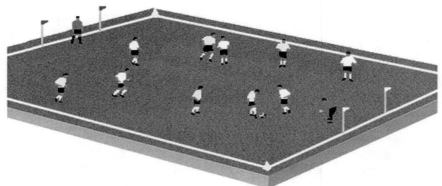

Finish with small sided game with goalkeepers.

Instructions:

The practice should be concluded with a small-sided game reinforcing the coaching points from your drills.

- Divide the players into two equal teams with goalkeepers.
- Each field should be approximately 40 yards x 60 yards.
- Use corner flags or cones as goals.
- Total time, 30 minutes.

At the end of your session, review all coaching points made during the practice.

Team 1 score _____ v Team 2 score _____

IMPORTANT ANNOUNCEMENTS FOR NEXT GAME/PRACTICE:

Getting behind the ball

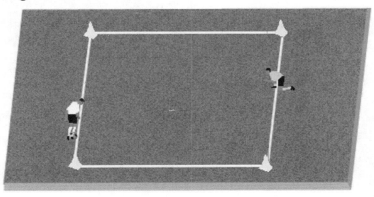

Objective:

This practice is designed to improve each player's ability in "ball control". The emphasis is placed on getting behind the flight of the ball early, so the player is composed and comfortable when controlling the ball.

Instructions:

Two players per grid, with one ball. The grid should be 10 yards x 10 yards. The players are positioned facing each other at each end of the grid. The player with the ball starts the practice by rolling the ball to the side of his partner and in between the cones. As the ball is traveling towards the receiving player, he must quickly get behind the flight of the ball and be in a balanced position ready to control it. The player must control the ball with feet and pass it back to his partner. The speed of the service should be increased gradually. Ensure that the ball is not rolled too close to the receiving player. Have the server aim for the inside of the cones.

The earlier a player gets behind the flight of the ball, the more time he will have to control it. Swap roles so each performs the drills.

Equipment:

Grid 10 yards by 10 yards
2 Players
1 Ball
4 Cones

Pass and receive

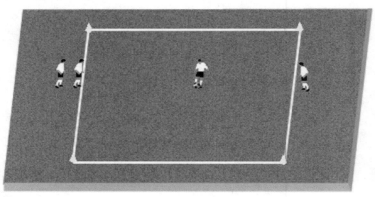

Objective:

This practice is designed to improve each player's ability to control a pass played on the ground.

Instructions:

Four players per grid, using one ball. The grid should be 10 yards x 20 yards. Three players are positioned at one side of the grid facing the server. The player with the ball starts the practice by passing the ball to the server. The player follows the pass and receives a return pass from the server. The receiving player must control the ball as economically as possible, turn and pass to the next player in sequence. The player then returns to the starting position and the practice is repeated.

The speed of the practice should be increased gradually.

The coach should emphasize the following coaching points:

- Demand the ball from the server. Call for the pass.
- Control and turn using either the inside or outside of the foot.
- Turn quickly and get the ball out of the feet.
- Try to turn and pass in two touches.

Equipment:

Grid 10 yards by 20 yards
4 Players
1 Ball
4 Cones

Wedge Control relay

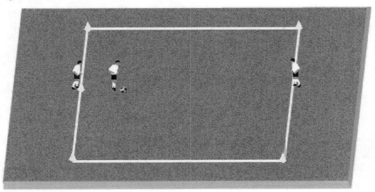

Objective:

This practice is designed to improve each player's ability to master the Wedge Control technique.

Instructions:

Three players per grid, using one ball. The grid should be 10 yards x 20 yards. Two players are positioned at one side of the grid facing the server. The first player runs towards the server and receives a pass into feet. The player must redirect the ball out of his feet on the first touch and pass the ball back to the server on their second touch. After passing the ball the player returns to his starting position. The practice is repeated with the next player.

The speed of the practice should be increased gradually.

The coach should emphasize the following coaching points:

- Demand the ball from the server. Call for the pass.
- Redirect the ball using either the inside or outside of the foot.
- Get the ball out of the feet far enough to pass comfortably on the second touch.
- Get the head up and scan the play as the ball is directed out of the feet.

Equipment:

Grid 10 yards by 20 yards
3 Players
1 Ball
4 Cones

Wedge Control in pairs

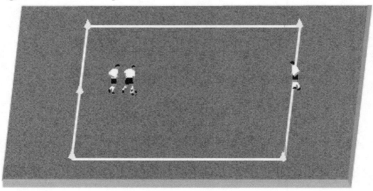

Objective:

This practice is designed to improve each player's ability to master the Wedge Control technique while under pressure.

Instructions:

Three players per grid, using one ball. The grid should be 10 yards x 20 yards. Two players are positioned at one side of the grid facing the server. The first player runs towards the server and receives a pass into feet. The second player follows the receiver and defends behind him. The first player must redirect the ball out of his feet on the first touch and pass the ball back to the server with the second touch. After passing the ball both players return to their starting position and reverse roles. The practice is repeated with the next player.

The speed of the practice should be increased gradually.

The coach should emphasize the following coaching points:

- Demand the ball from the server. Call for the pass.
- Redirect the ball using either the inside or outside of the foot.
- Get the ball out of the feet far enough to pass comfortably
  on the second touch.
- Get the head up and scan the play as the ball is
  directed out of the feet.
- Defender must be passive at first, then gradually
  increase pressure on the receiver.

Equipment:
Grid 10 yards by 20 yards
3 Players
1 Ball, 4 Cones

Small-Sided Game

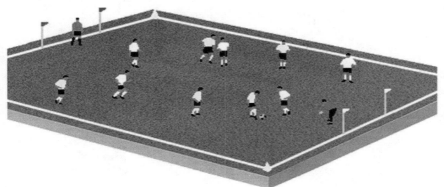

Finish with small sided game with goalkeepers.

Instructions:

The practice should be concluded with a small-sided game reinforcing the coaching points from your drills.

- Divide the players into two equal teams with goalkeepers.
- Each field should be approximately 40 yards x 60 yards.
- Use corner flags or cones as goals.
- Total time, 30 minutes.

At the end of your session, review all coaching points made during the practice.

Team 1 score _____ v Team 2 score _____

IMPORTANT ANNOUNCEMENTS FOR NEXT GAME/PRACTICE:

Control and Turn in the Grid

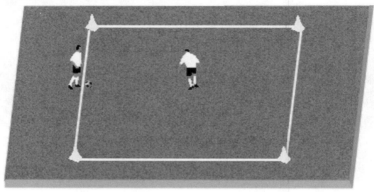

Objective:

This practice is designed to improve each player's controlling technique while turning with the ball.

Instructions:

Two players are positioned in a grid 10 yards x 10 yards. Each player has a ball. The first player starts the practice by playing the ball into the center of the grid. The player follows the pass, controls and turns as quickly as possible and returns to his starting position. His partner then repeats the practice.

The speed of the practice should be increased gradually.

The coach should emphasize the following coaching points:

- Pass the ball firmly into the center of the grid.
- Control and turn ball using either the inside or outside of the foot.
- Get the ball out of the feet far enough to enable to run comfortably in the intended direction.
- Get the head up and scan the play as the ball is directed out of the feet.

Equipment:

Grid 10 yards by 20 yards
2 Players
1 Ball per player
4 Cones

Wedge Relay turn in the Grid

Objective:
This practice is designed to improve each player's Wedge Control technique while turning with the ball.

Instructions:
Two players are positioned in a grid 10 yards x 10 yards. Each player has a ball. The first player starts the practice by throwing a looped serve into the center of the grid. The player follows the pass, controls and turns as quickly as possible and returns to his starting position. His partner then repeats the practice.

The speed of the practice should be increased gradually.

The coach should emphasize the following coaching points:

- Throw the ball high enough to make the practice challenging.
- Decide by the flight of the ball which surface of the foot is to be used in the wedge control (inside or outside of the foot).
- The ankle of the controlling foot should be firm and not relaxed.
- Immediately on impact, redirect the ball away from the body and into available space. Do not withdraw the ball into the body. The ball should be redirected, not cushioned.
- Get the ball out of the feet far enough to run comfortably in the intended direction.
- As the player is redirecting the ball on impact, the head and upper body should be over the ball.
- Get the head up and scan the play as the ball is directed out of the feet.

Equipment:
Grid 10 yards by 20 yards
2 Players,
1 Ball per player,
4 Cones

41

Rotary Thigh Control

Objective:
This practice is structured to improve the technical ability of the "Cushion Control using the Thigh".

Instructions:
Eight players are positioned in a grid 20 yards x 20 yards. One cone is placed in the center of the grid as a marker. Four players are positioned in the corners of the grid, each with a ball. Four players start from the center cone, each facing one of the servers. The players in the center of the grid receive a high looped throw from the server. The player must prevent the ball from hitting the ground using the Cushion Control with the Thigh. After controlling the ball the player must pass back to the server, check back to the center cone and repeat with the next server to the right. The players continue for approximately 3 minutes.

Emphasis should be placed on quality control. The pass should be played back at the correct pace so the receiver can control the ball with ease.

It is advised to have an extra ball at each cone to keep the tempo of the practice constant.
A point is scored for each control and pass completed. Each player should keep his own score.
A team total can be recorded to challenge the next set of four players.

Equipment:
Grid 20 yards by 20 yards   4 Balls or more
8 Players   9 Cones

Chest Rotary Drill

Objective:

This practice is structured to improve the technical ability of the "Cushion Control using the Chest".

Instructions:

Eight players are positioned in a grid 20 yards x 20 yards. One cone is placed in the center of the grid as a marker. Four players are positioned in the corners of the grid, each with a ball. Four players start from the center cone, each facing one of the servers. The players in the center of the grid receive a high looped throw from the server. The player must prevent the ball from hitting the ground using the Cushion Control with the Chest. After controlling the ball the player must pass back to the server, check back to the center cone and repeat with the next server to the right. The players continue for approximately 3 minutes.

Emphasis should be placed on quality control. The pass should be played back at the correct pace so the receiver can control the ball with ease.

It is advised to have an extra ball at each cone to keep the tempo of the practice constant.
A point is scored for each control and pass completed. Each player should keep his own score.
A team total can be recorded to challenge the next set of four players.

Equipment:

Grid 20 yards by 20 yards   4 Balls or more
8 Players   9 Cones

Small-Sided Game

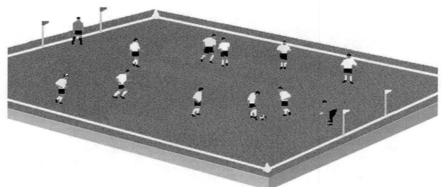

Finish with small sided game with goalkeepers.

Instructions:

The practice should be concluded with a small-sided game reinforcing the coaching points from your drills.

- Divide the players into two equal teams with goalkeepers.
- Each field should be approximately 40 yards x 60 yards.
- Use corner flags or cones as goals.
- Total time, 30 minutes.

At the end of your session, review all coaching points made during the practice.

Team 1 score _____ v Team 2 score _____

IMPORTANT ANNOUNCEMENTS FOR NEXT GAME/PRACTICE:

Shooting 2 v 1 Running Goalkeeper

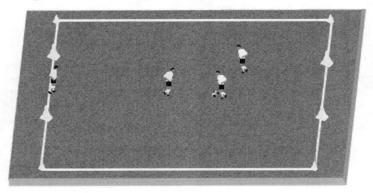

Objective:
This practice is designed to improve the player's technical ability in a variety of shooting techniques.

Instructions:
Two pairs of players are positioned in a grid 20 yards x 40 yards. Each team starts from their goal. One team starts with the ball, the other team on defense. The offensive team attacks with two players and attempts to score a goal. The defensive team plays with one defender and one goalkeeper. Only the goalkeeper may use his hands.

- If the attacking team scores, one attacker becomes a defender, the second must run behind the cones and into the goal to act as a goalkeeper.
- If the defending goalkeeper catches the ball, they now become the offensive team.
- If the defending player wins the ball, they now become the offensive team.
- When possession changes, the offensive team must counter as quickly as possible.
- The team who scores the most goals in 10 minutes wins, rotate groups to compete against different players.

Equipment:
Grid 20 yards by 40 yards
4 Players
Supply of balls
8 Cones

Shooting Center and Wide

Objective:

This practice is designed to improve the player's technical ability in a variety of shooting techniques.

Instructions:

A group of players are placed at the edge of the penalty area. Two servers are positioned each side of the goal. One server passes the ball to the edge of the box for the shooter to hit first time. Immediately after shooting the ball, the second server delivers a short-range pass at an angle from the goal for the shooter to strike. After taking both shots, the shooter returns to his staring position and joins the end of the line.

Coach should keep track of goals scored and make a competition amongst the shooters.

The coach should emphasize the following coaching points:

- The emphasis should be placed on "accuracy" and not power.
- Players should time their runs so that they do not have to break stride when striking the ball.
- Remember to keep the head steady and eyes fixed firmly on the ball.

Encourage players to use a variety of shooting techniques such as the low driven shot, the chip shot, the lofted shot and bent shot etc.

Equipment:

Penalty Area, Goal with net
Small group of players, 1 Goalkeeper, Supply of balls, 2 Cones

Give and Go edge of Box

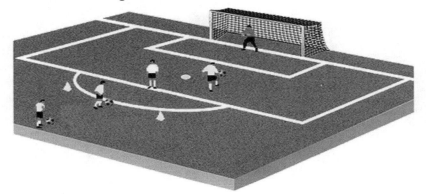

Objective:

This practice is designed to improve the player's technical ability in a variety of shooting techniques with an emphasis on the "give and go".

Instructions:

A small group of players are placed at the edge of the penalty area. One server is positioned at the edge of the penalty area. The first shooter in line passes the ball to the server for a return pass. The server passes either to his left or right for the shooter to hit first time. Immediately after shooting the ball the shooter must look to follow through for any rebounds from the goalkeeper. The shooter then returns to the starting position and joins the end of the line.

Coach should keep track of goals scored and make a competition amongst the shooters.

The coach should emphasize the following coaching points:

- The emphasis should be placed on "accuracy" and not power.
- Players should time their runs so that they do not have to break stride when striking the ball.
- Remember to keep the head steady and eyes fixed firmly on the ball.
- Encourage players to use a variety of shooting techniques such as the low driven shot, the chip shot, the lofted shot and bent shot etc.

Equipment:

Penalty Area, Goal with net
Small group of players, 1 Goalkeeper
Supply of balls
2 Cones

Shooting World Cup Drill

Objective:
This practice is designed to improve the player's technical ability in a variety of close range shooting techniques.

Instructions:
A group of players is divided equally into two groups. One group is positioned behind the goal to recover missed shots. The second group is split equally and positioned at two cones placed at the edge of the penalty area. Two servers, positioned each side of the goal, serve the ball on the ground and between the two cones placed approximately 12 yards from the goal line. Servers alternate.

Players recovering the balls must always ensure there is a ready supply of ball for the servers.

Players shooting must receive a pass from the server diagonally opposite. The ball must be struck after it passes through the cones. Any ball struck before passing through the cones does not count. The group works as a team to see how many goals they can score in three minutes. After the three minutes, all goals are totaled and the groups alternate.

The emphasis should be placed on "accuracy" and not power. Players should time their runs so that they do not have to break stride when striking the ball.

Equipment:
Penalty Area, Goal with net
Small group of players, 1 Goalkeeper
Supply of balls
4 Cones

Small-Sided Game

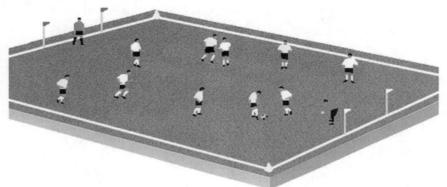

Finish with small sided game with goalkeepers.

Instructions:

The practice should be concluded with a small-sided game reinforcing the coaching points from your drills.

- Divide the players into two equal teams with goalkeepers.
- Each field should be approximately 40 yards x 60 yards.
- Use corner flags or cones as goals.
- Total time, 30 minutes.

At the end of your session, review all coaching points made during the practice.

Team 1 score _____ v Team 2 score _____

IMPORTANT ANNOUNCEMENTS FOR NEXT GAME/PRACTICE:

Heading for Distance

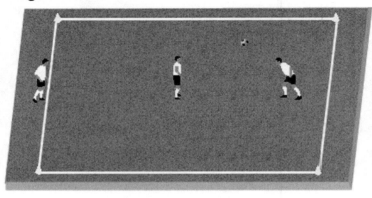

Objective:
This practice is designed to improve the mechanics involved when heading for distance.

Instructions:
Three players are positioned in a grid 10 yards x 20 yards. One player is placed on each side of the grid with the server positioned in the center. The server starts the practice by throwing the ball for one of the receivers to head. The receiver heads the ball above and beyond the server to the player at the opposite side of the grid. The second receiver heads the ball back to the server's hands to repeat the practice from that side.

The coach should emphasize the following coaching points:

- Ensure that the server delivers quality throws for heading.
- Attack the ball; don't wait for the ball to come to you.
- Get under the flight of the ball as early as possible for good balance.
- Remember to keep the head steady and eyes fixed firmly on the ball.
- Immediately on impact, the player should swing the upper body forward quickly and make contact on the ball with the center of the forehead.
- The player should redirect the ball with height and distance. Do not tilt the head too far back or the ball will skim from the head.

Equipment:
Grid 10 yards by 20 yards
3 Players
1 Ball
4 Cones

Heading Midfield Battles

Objective:

This practice is designed to improve defensive and offensive heading techniques in the midfield third.

Instructions:

Two groups of four players are positioned in the middle third of the field. Mark the middle third with cones. One group acts as defenders, the second as attackers. Two servers are placed in the six-yard box. The servers alternate playing long lofted passes into the middle third of the field.

The object of the practice is for both groups to challenge and win the header. The defensive team must head the ball back towards the servers and past the cones to win a point. The offensive team must try to "flick" the ball over the defenders and past the end cones to win a point.

Change roles so each group practices defensive and offensive heading.

The coach should emphasize the following coaching points:

- Ensure that the server delivers quality high lofted passes into the middle third.
- Attack the ball; don't wait for the ball to come to you.
- Get under the flight of the ball as early as possible for good balance.
- Remember to keep the head steady and eyes fixed firmly on the ball.
- Defensively: Immediately on impact, the player should swing the upper body forward quickly and make contact on the ball with the center of the forehead.
- The player should redirect the ball with height and distance.
- Do not tilt the head too far back or the ball will skim from the head.

51

- Offensively: Time your jumps carefully.
- On the approach to the ball, slightly arch the back and tighten the neck muscles.
- Contact is made with the top part of the forehead and below the horizontal mid-line of the ball. The ball should be redirected with just a small part of the ball glancing off the forehead. Immediately on making contact with the ball, the player should quickly swing the upper body and make contact on the ball with the center of the forehead.

Equipment:
Full size field
10 Players
Large supply of balls
10 Cones

World Cup Heading 2 v 2

Objective:

This practice is structured to improve the technical ability of "heading" with an emphasis on "accuracy and power".

Instructions:

Four players are positioned in a grid 8 yards x 7 yards, using one ball. The players are divided into teams of two. Both sets of players defend a goal marked by the cones. The players act as goalkeepers and may use their hands to stop a header. Goals are scored with a header between the cones and under head-height of the players.

The practice starts with one server throwing a straight throw from the nearest sideline for his partner to head at goal. The player heading the ball must head from the goal-line. The two goalkeepers must try to stop the header. When they catch the ball they also must serve from the nearest sideline and head at goal. The players must always keep the correct sequence; no player may have two headers in succession.

If a team defending can head the ball back at goal without first catching the ball they can score 2 points for a double header, 3 points for a triple header and so on. After the server throws the ball to his partner he must quickly return to his goal line to defend the goal. A supply of balls should be placed alongside the grid to maintain a high tempo. Encourage the players to attempt "Diving Headers" at goal when the opportunity presents itself.

Equipment:

Grid 8 yards by 7 yards
4 Players
4 Cones, 1 Ball

World Cup Heading at Goal

Objective:
This practice is designed to improve the player's technical ability in "heading".

Instructions:
Players are divided equally into two groups. One group is positioned behind the goal to recover missed headers. The second group is split equally and positioned at two cones placed at the edge of the penalty area. Two servers, positioned each side of the goal, serve the ball in the air and between the two cones placed approximately 12 yards from the goal line. Servers alternate.

Players recovering the balls must always ensure there is a ready supply of ball for the servers.

Players heading must receive a throw from the server diagonally opposite. The ball must be struck after it passes through the cones. Any ball struck before passing through the cones does not count. The group works as a team to see how many goals they can score in a three-minute period. After the three-minute period, all goals are totaled and groups alternate.

The emphasis should be placed on accuracy and power. Players should time their runs so that they do not have to break stride when heading the ball.

Equipment:
Penalty area, Goal with net
Small group of players,
1 goalkeeper,
Large supply of balls

Small-Sided Game

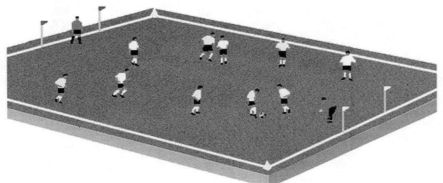

Finish with small sided game with goalkeepers.

Instructions:
The practice should be concluded with a small-sided game reinforcing the coaching points from your drills.

- Divide the players into two equal teams with goalkeepers.
- Each field should be approximately 40 yards x 60 yards.
- Use corner flags or cones as goals.
- Total time, 30 minutes.

At the end of your session, review all coaching points made during the practice.

Team 1 score _____ v Team 2 score _____

IMPORTANT ANNOUNCEMENTS FOR NEXT GAME/PRACTICE:

Defending 1 v 1

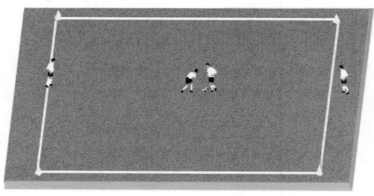

Objective:

This practice is designed to improve each player's one on one defending skills.

Instructions:

Two players are positioned on each side of a grid 10 yards x 20 yards. The player with the ball starts the practice by passing the ball to the first player at the opposite side of the grid. After passing the ball, the player immediately must defend the player receiving the ball. The player in possession must reach the opposite end line to score a point. The defender must win the ball to score a point. The next two players repeat the practice from the opposite side.

The speed of the practice should be increased gradually.

The coach should emphasize the following coaching points:

- Pass the ball firmly to the receiving player.
- Gain as much ground as possible as the ball is traveling.
- Slow down the last 2 yards. Get low with knees bent.
- Adopt a "side on" position.
- Make the direction of the play predictable.
- Timing of the tackle is important, wait for the forward to make his move.
- Quality tackling is as much an attitude as it is technique. Players must develop an aggressive and savvy attitude towards winning the ball.

Equipment:
Grid 10 yards by 20 yards
4 Players, 1 Ball, 4 Cones

Defending 1 v 2

Objective:
This practice is designed to improve each player's one on two defending skills.

Instructions:
Three players are positioned on each side of a grid 10 yards x 20 yards. The player with the ball starts the practice by passing the ball to the first two players at the opposite side of the grid. After passing the ball, the player immediately must defend against the two attackers. The attackers must reach the opposite end line to score a point. The defender must win the ball to score a point. Players repeat the practice from the opposite side.

The speed of the practice should be increased gradually.

The coach should emphasize the following coaching points:

- Pass the ball firmly to the receiving player.
- Gain as much ground as possible as the ball is traveling.
- Keep both attackers in view at all times.
- Slow down the last 2 yards. Get low with knees bent.
- Adopt a "side on" position.
- Make the direction of the play predictable.
- Timing of the tackle is important, wait for the forward to make his move.
- Quality tackling is as much an attitude as it is technique. Players must develop an aggressive and savvy attitude towards winning the ball.

Equipment:
Grid 10 yards by 20 yards
6 Players
1 Ball, 4 Cones

Defending 1 v 1 Swap Grid

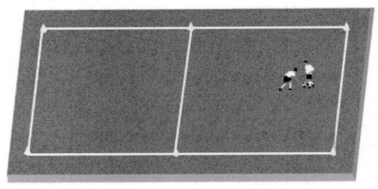

Objective:
This practice is designed to improve the player's one on one defending skills.

Instructions:
Two players are positioned in a grid 10 yards x 20 yards. The grid is divided into two smaller grids. To start the practice both players pass the ball around one of the grids. After several passes, one player plays the ball into the opposite grid for his partner to chase, control and turn. The player with the ball becomes the attacker and the other becomes the defender.

To score a point the attacker must get past the defender and stop the ball at the opposite end of the grid. The defender scores a point by winning the ball and running with it to the attackers end of the grid. The practice is repeated, alternating roles each time.

The speed of the practice should be increased gradually.

The coach should emphasize the following coaching points:

- Pass the ball firmly into the opposite grid.
- Gain as much ground as possible as the ball is traveling.
- Slow down the last 2 yards. Get low with knees bent.
- Prevent the attacker from turning whenever possible.
- Adopt a "side on" position.
- Make the direction of the play predictable.
- Timing of the tackle is important, wait for the forward to make his move.
- Quality tackling is as much an attitude as it is technique. Players must develop an aggressive and savvy attitude towards winning the ball.

Equipment:
Grid 10 yards by 20 yards
2 Players,
1 Ball,
6 Cones

Defending 1 v 1 around the Box

Objective:
This practice is designed to improve the player's one on one defending skills in and around the penalty area.

Instructions:
The defending group is positioned at the junction of the six-yard box and the end line.

The attacking group is placed on the sideline approximately 25 yards from the corner flag.

The practice starts when the first defender passes the ball to the first attacker. The defender must follow his pass and prevent the attacker from scoring a goal. A goal is also awarded each time the defender can successfully dispossess the attacker. After the play is completed, both players return to their starting positions. The next players in line repeat the practice.

Players should alternate the roles frequently. The speed of the practice should be increased gradually.

The coach should emphasize the following coaching points:

- Pass the ball firmly to the attacking player's feet.
- Gain as much ground as possible as the ball is traveling.
- Keep between the ball and the goal.
- Slow down the last 2 yards. Get low with knees bent.
- Adopt a "side on" position.
- Make the direction of the play predictable (away from the goal).
- Timing of the tackle is important, wait for the forward to make his move.
- Quality tackling is as much an attitude as it is technique. Players must develop an aggressive and savvy attitude towards winning the ball.

Equipment:
Penalty area
Goal with net
2 small groups
Large supply of balls,
4 Cones,
1 Corner flag

Small-Sided Game

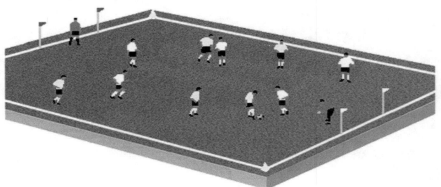

Finish with small sided game with goalkeepers.

Instructions:

The practice should be concluded with a small-sided game reinforcing the coaching points from your drills.

- Divide the players into two equal teams with goalkeepers.
- Each field should be approximately 40 yards x 60 yards.
- Use corner flags or cones as goals.
- Total time, 30 minutes.

At the end of your session, review all coaching points made during the practice.

Team 1 score _____ v Team 2 score _____

IMPORTANT ANNOUNCEMENTS FOR NEXT GAME/PRACTICE:

Explosive Body Movements

Objective:
This practice is designed to improve the technical ability of explosive body movements, feints and dribbling moves.

Instructions:
Two cones should be placed approximately 10 yards apart. Two players are positioned each side of the cones. No player may cross over the imaginary line and the defender may not try to steal the ball.

The player in possession of the ball must use body feints, head fakes and a variety of dribbling moves to upset the balance of the defender. A goal is scored each time the dribbling player can lose the defender and stop the ball dead at either of the cones. The dribbling player's knees should be bent and center of gravity low for an explosive start. If the defender does not move by using body movements, then move the ball to move the position of the defender. Once the defender is off balance the attacker should explode into the opposite direction. Try to face the defender at all times.

The defensive player can prevent the dribbling player from scoring a goal by placing his foot in front of the cone the player is attacking. The defender may not tackle or cross over the imaginary line. Players should alternate every 3 minutes. Score should be kept to determine winner.

Equipment:
2 Cones 10 yards apart
2 Players,
1 Ball

Dribbling Slalom through Cones

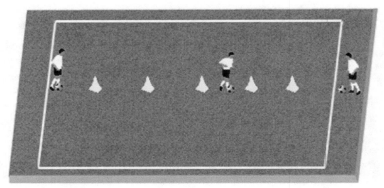

Objective:
This practice is designed to develop close control while running with the ball.

Instructions:
Two players are positioned at one end of the grid, with one player at the opposite side. Players alternate dribbling the ball at full speed through the line of cones. Cones are placed at 1-yard intervals across the full length of the grid.

Equipment:
Grid 10 yards by 5 yards
3 Players or more
1 Ball per player
Minimum of 5 cones

Dribble, Turn and Escape

Objective:

This practice is designed to develop close control while running and turning with the ball.

Instructions:

Divide players into pairs, with one ball each. Players alternate dribbling the ball towards each other. At the mid-point of the grid, players turn and dribble back to their starting positions. Players should accelerate after turning.

Equipment:

Grid 10 yards by 5 yards
2 Players or more
1 Ball per player
6 Cones

Dribbling 1v1

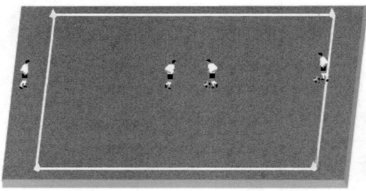

Objective:

This practice is designed to improve each player's one on one dribbling skills.

Instructions:

Two players are positioned on each side of a grid 10 yards x 20 yards. The player with the ball starts the practice by passing the ball to the first player at the opposite side of the grid. After passing the ball, the player immediately must defend the player receiving the ball. Using a variety of dribbling techniques the player in possession must reach the opposite end line to score a point. The next two players then repeat the practice from the opposite side.

The speed of the practice should be increased gradually.

The coach should emphasize the following coaching points:

- Control the ball quickly.
- Attack the defender with speed. Don't delay the attack.
- Commit the defender by running at him.
- Disguise your intentions through body fakes, head feints and moving
  the ball.

Equipment:

Grid 10 yards by 20 yards
4 Players
2 Balls
4 Cones

Small-Sided Game

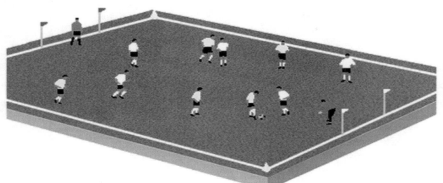

Finish with small sided game with goalkeepers.

Instructions:
The practice should be concluded with a small-sided game reinforcing the coaching points from your drills.

- Divide the players into two equal teams with goalkeepers.
- Each field should be approximately 40 yards x 60 yards.
- Use corner flags or cones as goals.
- Total time, 30 minutes.

At the end of your session, review all coaching points made during the practice.

Team 1 score _____ v Team 2 score _____

IMPORTANT ANNOUNCEMENTS FOR NEXT GAME/PRACTICE:

Chapter 2

Learn the Skills

The most singular important factor in winning games is not tactics or formations, it is the quality of individual "technique". Team tactics are totally dependent upon each player's ability to execute the technical components of those tactics. For tactics to succeed you must have players who can pass the ball diagonally behind a defense, control the ball in tight areas, dribble past an opponent, or win head balls in set-plays.

Without players who possess good technique, your time invested in team organization and principles of play will be fruitless. With players of high technical ability, the foundation will be strong to apply those techniques in skillful and tactical situations.

It is of paramount importance that coaches understand how quality technique is developed and implement a coaching regimen to challenge players to a level of technical excellence.

"Practice does not make perfect". Rather, "practice makes permanent." To teach technique, coaches must be able to break down each component and relay that information to their players. The technique must be isolated and performed until it becomes habit. This section will provide detailed coaching points for developing high levels of technique.

Passing

There are twelve surfaces on the feet in which a player can pass a ball, six surfaces on the right foot and six on the left foot.

These surfaces are:

- The inside of the foot
- The outside of the foot
- The instep of the foot
- The toe
- The heel of the foot
- The sole of the foot

Moreover, a player can also opt to pass a ball:

- Over a short distance
- Over a long distance
- On the ground
- In the air

There are several components that will affect the quality and success of each pass, in sequence, these are:

- Selection of passing technique
- Disguising the intentions of the pass
- Timing of the pass
- Speed or weight of the pass
- Accuracy of the pass

There are 16 types of passing techniques to master:

- The Push Pass
- The Low Driven Pass
- The Lofted Pass
- The Chip Pass
- The Bent or Swerved Pass
- The Volley Pass
- The Half Volley Pass
- The Toe Poke Pass
- The Heel Pass
- The Sole of the Foot Pass
- The Flick Pass
- The Stab Pass
- Pass using the Head
- Pass using the Chest
- Pass using the Thigh
- Throw-ins

Step One:
Approach the ball at a slight angle. Place your non-kicking foot along-side the ball, not so close that it will prevent the natural swinging motion of the kicking leg. The ankle of the kicking foot must be firm. Use a slight drawback of the kicking foot.

Step Two:
Strike the ball with the inside of the kicking foot through the horizontal mid-line of the ball. The head should be kept steady and eyes fixed firmly on the ball. The head weighs approximately 10 pounds, so any unnecessary tilting of the head will affect the whole balance of the body.

Step Three:
The follow through is in the direction of the intended target.

Step One:
Approach the ball at a slight angle. This will assist the natural swinging motion of the kicking leg. The head should be kept steady and eyes fixed firmly on the ball. The head weighs approximately 10 pounds, so any unnecessary tilting of the head will affect the whole balance of the body. The non-kicking foot should be placed alongside and slightly in front of the ball.

Step Two:
Contact on the ball with the kicking foot should be made through the horizontal mid-line of the ball. The kicking foot should be fully extended down and the ball should be struck with the laces of the boot.

Step Three:
The follow through should be made through the center of the ball and continue in the direction of the intended target.

Step One:
Approach the ball at a slight angle. This will assist the natural swinging motion of the kicking leg. The head should be kept steady with eyes fixed firmly on the ball. Plant the non-kicking foot alongside and slightly in front of the ball. The head and upper body should be over the ball. Withdrawal with the kicking leg is predominantly from the knee and not the hip.

Step Two:
Contact on the ball should be made through the underside and center of the ball. Using a stabbing action from the knee and not the hip, strike down onto the underside of the ball, as to impart a vicious backspin on the ball. The more powerful the stabbing action of the kicking foot down onto the ball, the more rapidly the ball will climb with a quality backspin.

Step Three:
The backspin of the ball is necessary to allow the ball to stop within a short distance, after making contact with the ground.

Step One:
Approach the ball at an angle. This will assist in the natural swinging motion of the kicking leg. The head should be kept steady and eyes fixed firmly on the ball. The last stride on the approach to the ball should be the longest. This will increase the length of the back swing from the kicking leg. Plant the non-kicking foot alongside and slightly behind the ball. Do not position the non-kicking foot too close to the ball as to interfere with the natural swinging motion of the kicking leg.

Step Two:
Contact with the kicking foot on the ball is made with the instep. The ball should be struck through the center and on the under side of the ball, where the ball rests on the surface of the ground. Withdrawal from the kicking leg comes from the hip as well as the knee for extra power and distance.

Step Three:
The follow through is long and continues through the ball into the direction of the intended target. There is hardly any backspin on the ball, thus allowing the ball to roll as it makes contact with the ground.

The Bent Pass

Step One:
Approach the ball at a slight angle. This will assist the natural swinging motion of the kicking leg. The head should be kept steady and eyes fixed firmly on the ball. Plant the non-kicking foot approximately 10 inches away to the side of the ball.

Step Two:
Contact with the kicking foot is made with the instep. The point of contact on the ball should be slightly below the horizontal mid-line and to the side of the ball. If contact is made too close to the center of the ball, then the ball will not spin. Too little contact on the ball will result in the ball being sliced.

Step Three:
Unlike other passes, the follow through of the kicking foot travels away from the direction of the ball. The above mechanics also apply to bending the ball with the outside of the foot.

Step One:

Approach the ball straight on. This will assist in the natural swinging motion of the kicking leg. The head should be kept steady and eyes fixed firmly on the ball. Plant the non-kicking foot alongside and parallel with the ball. Do not position the non-kicking foot too close to the ball as to interfere with the natural swinging motion of the kicking leg.

Raise the kicking foot over the top of the ball to disguise your intentions. Continue over the ball and make contact on the front of the ball with the heel.

Step Two:

The ball should be struck through the center and on the horizontal mid-line of the ball. Withdrawal from the kicking leg comes from the hip as well as the knee.

Step Three:

The follow through is short and continues slightly through the ball into the direction of the intended target.

The Stab Pass

Step One:
Approach the ball straight on. Keep the head steady and eyes fixed firmly on the ball. Plant the non-kicking foot to the side of the ball. Withdrawal from the kicking leg is made from the knee and not from the hip.

Step Two:
Contact with the kicking foot is made with the outside front of the shoe. Contact on the ball is made through the horizontal mid-line of the ball. Withdraw the foot and with a quick stab of the foot and contact through the center of the ball.

Step Three:
The follow through is short and in the direction of the intended target.

Ball Control

Players must understand that ball control is not a means in itself, but a means to and end.
At the end of each control a player will have four options to act on:

- Most often the player will control to pass the ball.
- In the attacking third players will control to set up shots.
- The player may control the ball to dribble.
- The player may control to run with the ball.

With this is mind, the player should decide as the ball is in flight what he intends to do after controlling the ball: is he going to pass, shoot, dribble or run with the ball. The quality of the player's first touch on the ball will often determine the quality of the action that follows.

Many coaches instruct players to "trap the ball" before passing it. The word "trap" suggests stopping the ball. Young players get into a bad habit of trapping the ball using the sole of the foot every time the ball comes to them. Trapping or stopping the ball with the sole of the foot can cause many bad habits for the player and limit the techniques he can use immediately after his first touch on the ball.

The following are bad habits as a result of "trapping the ball" with the sole of the foot:

- As the ball travels towards the foot the head will drop and eyes will be fixed on the ball. The player at this point cannot see his passing options.

- In the attacking third, the player will not be able to see the position of the goalkeeper if his head is down, thus limiting his shooting options.

- If the ball is controlled with the sole of the foot on the first touch, the position of the ball will be too close to the player's body for the player to pass over a long distance. There needs to be a distance between the player and the ball for the player to strike the ball over a long distance.

- In the attacking third, the player cannot afford to stop the ball with the sole of the foot. The player needs to set up shooting opportunities as soon as possible. If the ball is controlled with the sole of the foot, it will limit the player's ability to shoot over a long distance.

- Trapping the ball with the sole of the foot will also effect the time in which a player makes decisions. The player will take one second to trap the ball, another second to push the ball out from the body and yet a third second before the player considers the option of whether to pass, dribble, shoot or run with the ball. During this period the nearest opponent will be closing down the ball and looking to dispossess the player.

Coaches should encourage players to use their first touch on the ball economically and effectively. As opposed to trapping the ball with the sole of the foot, players should look to play their first touch out of their body and into a position that will allow them to perform a variety of techniques on their second touch.

In general, right-footed players should look to play their first touch approximately one and a half yards in front and to the right side at a 45-degree angle (left footed players to the left side).
By playing the ball out and in front of the body on the first touch, the player will improve in the following:

- Better all round vision as eyes follow ball out and up and not focused down at the feet.
- Can immediately evaluate passing and shooting options.
- Can pass the ball over a long range.
- Can shoot the ball over a long range.
- Less chance of being caught in possession of the ball due to improved vision.

During the course of a game it is not always possible to play the ball in the perfect position. However, it is surprising to note that on numerous occasions when players control the ball, they neglect to consider what they are controlling for, to pass, to shoot, to dribble or to run with the ball.

Players should play their first touch out and in front at a 45-degree angle.

There are four main controlling surfaces of the body, these are:

1. The head.
2. The chest.
3. The thighs.
4. The feet.

There are two types of ball control. These are the cushion control and the wedge control. Both of these can be performed on the head, chest, thighs or feet. The main differences between the cushion and the wedge control are:

The Cushion Control:

A player will normally select to use the cushion control when time and space are available. On making contact with the ball, the player will immediately withdraw the controlling surface of the head, chest, thigh or feet. This will take away from the power of the ball and act as a cushioning effect. The muscles in the body should be relaxed, thus making them soft for better surface to cushion the ball.

The Wedge Control:

A player should select the wedge control when time and space is limited. On making contact with the ball, the player will immediately push out and redirect the ball using the head, chest, thighs or feet. The muscles in the controlling surface should be tense and hard, thus making a better surface for the ball to redirect from.

Note:
It is recommended that a little air be taken out of the ball, to make the ball softer and easier to control. Young players will be less reluctant to control a soft ball than a hard ball. Try to use a hand-stitched ball and not plastic molded balls. Plastic balls are very difficult to control, especially on the chest, head and thigh.

Cushion Control using the Foot

Step One:
Position the body behind the flight of the ball as early as possible. This will lead to good composure and balance for receiving the ball instead of reaching out and being caught off balance. Decide by the flight of the ball which foot should be used. Remember to keep the head steady and eyes fixed firmly on the ball. The head weighs approximately 10 pounds, so any unnecessary tilting of the head will affect the whole balance of the body.

Step Two:
Offer the controlling surface of the foot to the ball (laces or the inside of the foot). Immediately withdraw the foot on impact of the ball. This will have a cushioning effect and kill the power of the ball. If the foot is not withdrawn quickly enough, the ball will bounce away from the player.

Step Three:
In a well-executed cushion control the ball should lie close to the controlling surface.

Step One:
Position the body behind the flight of the ball as early as possible. This will lead to good composure and balance for receiving the ball instead of reaching out and being caught off balance. Decide by the flight of the ball which thigh should be used to control the ball. Offer the controlling surface of the thigh to the ball.

Step Two:
Immediately withdraw the thigh on impact of the ball. This will have a cushioning effect and kill the power of the ball. If the thigh is not withdrawn quickly enough, the ball will bounce away from the player. When controlling the ball, try to position the thigh in front of the upper body and not extended out to the side of the body. This will block the ball should it bounce up off the thigh. If the thigh is extended to the side, then the ball may skim off the thigh and possession will be lost.

Step Three:
Remember to keep the head steady and eyes fixed firmly on the ball. In a well-executed cushion control the ball should lie close to the body.

Cushion Control using the Chest

Step One:
Position the body behind the flight of the ball as early as possible.
Remember to keep the head steady and eyes fixed firmly on the ball.
Offer the surface of the chest to the ball.
Off center of the chest will provide the best surface for the cushion control, due to the softness of the chest muscles.

Step Two:
Immediately withdraw the chest on impact of the ball. This will have a cushioning effect and kill the power of the ball. If the chest is not withdrawn quickly enough, the ball will bounce away from the player. The chest should be slightly tilted back, so when the ball contacts the chest, it will bounce up fractionally before dropping to the player's feet.

Step Three:
The knees should also be bent and withdrawn as soon as contact is made with the ball. In a well-executed cushion control the ball should lie close to the body.

Cushion Control using the Head

Step One:
Position the body behind the flight of the ball as early as possible. This will lead to good composure and balance for receiving the ball instead of reaching out and being caught off balance. Remember to keep the head steady and eyes fixed firmly on the ball.

Slightly lift up the chin and tilt back the surface of the forehead. Offer the surface of the forehead to the ball. The chest should be slightly tilted back and knees should be bent.

Step Two:
Immediately withdraw the head and bend the knees on impact of the ball. This will have a cushioning effect on the ball and kill the power of the ball. If the head and knees are not withdrawn quickly enough, the ball will bounce away from the player.

Step Three:
Do not tilt the head too far back or the ball will skim off the forehead and away from the player.
In a well-executed cushion control the ball should lie close to the body.

Wedge Control using the Foot

Step One:
Position the body behind the flight of the ball as early as possible. This will lead to good composure and balance for receiving the ball instead of reaching out and being caught off balance. Remember to keep the head steady and eyes fixed firmly on the ball.

Decide by the flight of the ball which surface of the foot is to be used in the wedge control (inside or outside of the foot).

Step Two:
The ankle of the controlling foot should be firm and not relaxed. Offer the controlling surface of the foot to the ball. Immediately on impact, redirect the ball away from the body and into available space. Do not withdraw the ball into the body. The ball should be redirected, not cushioned.

Step Three:
As the player is redirecting the ball on impact, the head and upper body should be over the ball.

Step One:
Position the body behind the flight of the ball as early as possible. This will lead to good composure and balance for receiving the ball instead of reaching out and being caught off balance. Remember to keep the head steady and eyes fixed firmly on the ball. The head weighs approximately 10 pounds, so any unnecessary tilting of the head will affect the whole balance of the body.

Step Two:
Decide by the flight of the ball which thigh is to be used to control the ball. The thigh muscle should be tight to provide a hard surface for redirecting the ball. Offer the controlling surface of the thigh to the ball.

Step Three:
Immediately on impact, push out with the thigh and redirect the ball into available space. Do not withdraw the thigh on impact, as this will cushion the ball. As the player is redirecting the ball on impact, the head and upper body should be over the ball.

Step One:
Position the body behind the flight of the ball as early as possible. This will lead to good composure and balance for receiving the ball instead of reaching out and being caught off balance. Remember to keep the head steady and eyes fixed firmly on the ball. The head weighs approximately 10 pounds, so any unnecessary tilting of the head will affect the whole balance of the body.

Step Two:
The chest should be tight with the shoulders pulled back. The player should also lean backwards slightly. Contact on the ball should be made with the center of the chest, as the sternum will provide a harder surface for the ball to rebound from.

Step Three:
Immediately on impact, quickly push the ball out from the chest and into available space. Do not withdraw the chest on impact, as this will cushion the ball. As the player is redirecting the ball on impact, the upper body should be forward with shoulders pinned back.

Wedge Control using the Head

Step One:
Position the body behind the flight of the ball as early as possible. This will lead to good composure and balance for receiving the ball instead of reaching out and being caught off balance. Remember to keep the head steady and eyes fixed firmly on the ball.

Step Two:
The player should lean forward with the head straight and the neck muscles tight. Contact on the ball should be made with the forehead. The forehead is the flattest and hardest part of the skull. This will assist in redirecting the ball.

Step Three:
Immediately on impact, the player should swing the upper body forward quickly and make contact on the ball with the center of the forehead. The player should redirect the ball into available space. Do not withdraw on impact, this will cushion the ball. Do not tilt the head too far back or the ball will skim from the head and possession may be lost. As the player is redirecting the ball on impact, the upper body and head should be moving forward.

Shooting

There can be no doubt that shooting is the most important aspect of attacking play. Everything you do as an individual and as a team is a means to the end, scoring goals.

- Players should possess a wide range of shooting techniques regardless of position.

- Sufficient time and effort should be given in practice for the improvement of finishing.

- Often players lack responsibility for shooting, either they will pass to a teammate or not shoot at all. Accepting personal responsibilities for goal scoring, as well as missing, is fundamental to becoming a consistent and confident goal scorer.

- Between passing, dribbling or shooting - shooting will bring the highest level of success in and around the penalty area. You should discourage yourself from making inter-passing movements in the attacking third when a shooting possibility arises.

- It is an obvious fact that there will be more occasions when we will miss the goal when shooting rather than score. It is estimated that only one out of every five shots will be converted.

- It is a lesser sin to shoot wide than high. A shot going wide may have some chance of a deflection, a shot going high merely gives the opposition a goal kick.

- A low shot has far more potential than a shot struck high at goal. In going for a high shot you are offering the goalkeeper a greater chance of stopping the ball. Moreover, shots along the ground may be deflected by another player, or may stick, bump or skip depending upon the playing surface.

- Shots going away from the goalkeeper to the far post are usually more difficult to save than shots to the near post. Not only are they difficult for the goalkeeper to hold, but the possibility of a deflection into a teammate's path is encouraging.

- We can define that goals are scored from three types of shots. These are balls moving towards the body, balls moving away from the body and balls moving across the body.

Inside of the Foot Shot

Step One:
Approach the ball at a slight angle. Place your non-kicking foot alongside the ball, not so close that it will prevent the natural swinging motion of the kicking leg. The ankle of the kicking foot must be firm. Use a slight drawback of the kicking foot.

Step Two:
Strike the ball with the inside of the kicking foot through the horizontal mid-line of the ball. The head should be kept steady and eyes fixed firmly on the ball. The head weighs approximately 10 pounds, so any unnecessary tilting of the head will affect the whole balance of the body.

Step Three:
The follow through is in the direction of the intended target.

Step One:
Approach the ball at a slight angle. This will assist the natural swinging motion of the kicking leg. The head should be kept steady and eyes fixed firmly on the ball. The head weighs approximately 10 pounds, so any unnecessary tilting of the head will affect the whole balance of the body.
The non-kicking foot should be placed alongside and slightly in front of the ball.

Step Two:
Contact on the ball with the kicking foot should be made though the horizontal mid-line of the ball. The kicking foot should be fully extended down and the ball should be struck with the laces of the boot.

Step Three:
The follow through should be made through the center of the ball and continue in the direction of the intended target.

The Chip Shot

Step One:
Approach the ball at a slight angle. This will assist the natural swinging motion of the kicking leg. The head should be kept steady with eyes fixed firmly on the ball. Plant the non-kicking foot alongside and slightly in front of the ball. The head and upper body should be over the ball. Withdrawal with the kicking leg is predominantly from the knee and not the hip.

Step Two:
Contact on the ball should be made through the underside and center of the ball. Using a stabbing action from the knee and not the hip, strike down onto the underside of the ball, as to impart a vicious backspin on the ball. The more powerful the stabbing action of the kicking foot down onto the ball, the more rapidly the ball will climb with a quality backspin.

Step Three:
The backspin of the ball is necessary to allow the ball to stop within a short distance, after making contact with the ground.

The Lofted Shot

Step One:
Approach the ball at an angle. This will assist in the natural swinging motion of the kicking leg. The head should be kept steady and eyes fixed firmly on the ball. The last stride on the approach to the ball should be the longest. This will increase the length of the back swing from the kicking leg. Plant the non-kicking foot alongside and slightly behind the ball. Do not position the non-kicking foot too close to the ball as to interfere with the natural swinging motion of the kicking leg.

Step Two:
Contact with the kicking foot on the ball is made with the instep. The ball should be struck through the center and on the under side of the ball, where the ball rests on the surface of the ground. Withdrawal from the kicking leg comes from the hip as well as the knee for extra power and distance.

Step Three:
The follow through is long and continues through the ball into the direction of the intended target. There is hardly any backspin on the ball, thus allowing the ball to roll as it makes contact with the ground.

Step One:
Approach the ball at a slight angle. This will assist the natural swinging motion of the kicking leg. The head should be kept steady and eyes fixed firmly on the ball. Plant the non-kicking foot approximately 10 inches away to the side of the ball.

Step Two:
Contact with the kicking foot is made with the instep. The point of contact on the ball should be slightly below the horizontal mid-line and to the side of the ball. If contact is made too close to the center of the ball, then the ball will not spin. Too little contact on the ball will result in the ball being sliced.

Step Three:
Unlike other passes, the follow through of the kicking foot travels away from the direction of the ball. The above mechanics also apply to bending the ball with the outside of the foot.

Volley Shot

Step One:
Players must always be alert to strike aerial balls in and around the penalty area. When using the front volley shot, the player should allow the ball to drop to a height slightly below the knee. If the player tries to strike the ball too high, this will undoubtedly result in a missed shot. On the approach, the player must step into the ball with the non-kicking foot. The head should be kept steady and eyes fixed firmly on the ball.

Step Two:
As the ball drops, contact with the kicking foot is made with the laces, and the foot should be fully extended down. Contact on the ball should be made slightly above the horizontal mid-line of the ball.

Step Three:
The power of the shot comes from a stabbing action from the knee and not the hip.

Step One:
Watch the flight of the ball carefully. On the approach, the player must step into the ball with the non-kicking foot. The head should be kept steady and eyes fixed firmly on the ball. When using the half volley shot, the player should allow the ball to hit the ground for a fraction of a second.

Step Two:
As the ball rises from the ground, approximately 4 inches, the ball is struck through the horizontal mid-line. Contact with the kicking foot is made with the laces and the foot should be fully extended down.

Step Three:
The power of the shot comes from a stabbing action from the knee and not the hip.

Heading

As defending has become more organized in modern soccer, the ground route for passing the ball has been reduced. With reduced passing space, high balls into the penalty area increases. During the course of a game the situations in which a player has to head the ball either for defensive or attacking purposes will be numerous.

Careful attention should be given to train players to deal with the physical and mental aspects of heading the ball. In fact, early experiences in heading the ball can be painful if careful progression in building up confidence is not applied.

Young players fear heading the ball because they feel it will harm them. Confidence has to be built slowly through correct repetition and encouragement. With this in mind we should examine the basic techniques involved in successful heading.

Heading is divided into two categories. "Defensive" heading and "Attacking" heading.

It is important in both defending and attacking that the player is first to the ball and prepared to attack it. The movement of the trunk backward and forwards, along with the neck muscles provide the power. The forehead is used because it is the flattest and thickest area of the head and gives a more accurate striking surface. On contact with the ball it is important that the player head through the ball in the direction of the intended target.

For defensive heading, follow three rules:

Head the ball high
Heading the ball high favors the defense as it allows them time to readjust their defensive positions and reorganize.

Head the ball long
Heading the ball long will help keep the ball away from immediate danger.

Head the ball wide
Heading the ball wide will play the ball into a safe angle from goal.

To execute these principals it is important to head the ball beneath the mid-line of the ball.

For attacking heading the key factor is keeping the ball low. Heading through the horizontal mid-line or top half of the ball enables you to head down towards the goal line, making it as difficult as possible for the goalkeeper.

In both defensive and attacking heading aggression and timing is of paramount importance.

Step One:
Get behind the flight of the ball. The player's eyes should be fixed on the flight of the ball.
On the approach to the ball, the player must slightly arch the back and tighten the neck muscles.

Step Two:
Immediately on making contact with the ball, the player should quickly swing the upper body and make contact on the ball with the center of the forehead. Further power can be achieved by pulling the arms back when making contact with the ball. Contact should be made above the horizontal mid-line of the ball. This will direct the ball downwards.

Step Three:
When heading for goal, the ball should be headed down towards the goal line. The timing of the run must be late, fast and aggressive.

Step One:
The player should position his body behind the flight of the ball as early as possible. This will provide good composure and balance to attack the ball. The eyes should be fixed on the flight of the ball, the back should be arched and neck muscle's tightened. The legs should be slightly bent, ready to extend when contact is made with the ball.

Step Two:
Contact is made with the center of the forehead and should be made through the center and below the horizontal mid-line of the ball. Immediately on making contact with the ball, the player should quickly swing the upper body forward. The legs should be positioned one behind the other for extra balance. By pulling the arms back when making contact, more power can be achieved.

Step Three:
When heading the ball defensively, the player should aim for distance, width and height. It is important for the player to develop an aggressive attitude towards defensive heading to win air balls consistently.

Step One:
The players eyes should be fixed on the flight of the ball. Get behind the flight of the ball.
On the approach to the ball, the player must slightly arch the back and tighten the neck muscles.

Step Two:
Contact is made with the top part of the forehead and below the horizontal mid-line of the ball. The ball should be redirected with just a small part of the ball glancing off the forehead.

Step Three:
Immediately on making contact with the ball, the player should quickly swing the upper body and make contact on the ball with the center of the forehead.

This Flick On header is most commonly used to redirect near post corner kicks and free kicks.
It is also used in the midfield and frontline when competing for headers from goal kicks.

Step One:
Get inline with the flight of the ball. The knees should be bent with hands extended. Lean forward into the direction of the ball. The forehead should be tilted back to enable the player to see the ball and to ensure contact with the forehead and the center of the ball.

Step Two:
Contact is made with the center of the forehead and should be made through the horizontal mid-line of the ball. This will direct the ball forward.

Step Three:
Power in a diving header is achieved by the timing and speed of the player's run into the flight of the ball. It is important that the player develop a brave and aggressive attitude towards diving headers to become a consistent opportunist.

Passing with the Head

Step One:
Position the body behind the flight of the ball as early as possible. This will lead to good composure and balance for receiving the ball instead of reaching out and being caught off balance. Remember to keep the head steady and eyes fixed firmly on the ball.

Step One:
Immediately on impact, the player should swing the upper body forward quickly and make contact on the ball with the center of the forehead. The player should redirect the ball to the player.
Do not withdraw on impact, this will cushion the ball. Do not tilt the head too far back or the ball will skim from the head and possession may be lost.

Step Three:
As the player is redirecting the ball, the upper body and head should be moving forward.

Dribbling

Where should players dribble?

The Attacking Third:

This is the arena for dribbling. In the attacking third of the field players must be encouraged to run at defenders with the ball. Creativity will pay big dividends if successful.

The Mid-field Third:

Mid-field players are often required to dribble to shake off tight markers or run with the ball on quick attacks. Each mid- fielder should possess at least one trick. Dribbling in the mid-field should only be used when good passing options are not available.

The Defensive Third:

On occasion defenders are also required to dribble to escape from tight situations. Dribbling in the defensive third should be kept to a minimum and executed with caution.

When should players dribble?

As a rule, players should only consider dribbling when there is a lack of quality support from team mates. If good support play is available, then passing should take priority.

Why should players dribble?

Explosive dribbling upsets the balance of the opponent's defensive structure. The unpredictability of dribbling often creates passing and shooting opportunities. If performed well and with discipline, dribbling can be the most entertaining of all soccer skills.

The Half Turn

Step One:
Place the sole of the foot on the ball. Drag the ball back behind you using the sole of the foot. Spin quickly on the standing foot (like an ice-skater on ice) turning 180 degrees towards the ball.

Step Two:
Push the ball far enough (approximately 1 yard) out of your feet to enable you to turn without taking a second touch.

Step Three:
The second touch should be to set up a pass, shot or dribble.

Step One:
The player should place the sole of the foot on the ball, toe turned inward and heel facing outward.

Step Two:
The player then drags the ball away from the standing foot and removes the foot off the ball.

Step Three:
Spinning quickly on the standing foot (like an ice-skater on ice) the player turns towards the ball as he redirects the ball at a 90 degree angle using the inside of the foot. Play the ball in the direction you want to travel.

The Beardsley

Step One:
Place the non-kicking foot slightly behind and to the side of the ball. Bend the knee of the kicking foot. With the lace of the shoe facing the ball, fake to play the ball past the non-kicking foot.

Step Two:
Quickly reverse the direction of the kicking foot and move the ball in the opposite direction of the standing foot. The head should be kept steady and eyes fixed firmly on the ball.

Step Three:
Play the ball in the direction you want to travel.

The Stop and Go

Step One:
Move alongside the ball. As the ball is traveling, stop the ball with the sole of the foot.
Withdraw the kicking foot behind the ball.

Step Two:
Push the ball forward using the laces of the same foot. Keep the toe pointing down all the way through the follow-through.

Step Three:
Lean forward slightly when executing the move and accelerate explosively.

The Fake Stop and Go

Step One:
Move alongside the ball. Fake over the ball pretending to back heel the ball and pull the foot back behind the ball.

Step Two:
Push the ball forward using the laces of the same foot.

Step Three:
Keep the toe pointing down all the way through the follow-through. Lean forward slightly when executing the move and accelerate explosively in the opposite direction.

The Step Over

Step One:
Move alongside the ball and approach the ball straight on. Plant the non-kicking foot alongside and parallel to the ball. Transfer your body weight onto the standing foot.

Step Two:
Bring the kicking foot over the top of the ball and plant the foot to the side of the ball.

Step Three:
Transfer your weight onto the foot and spin in the direction of the ball. Play the ball out of the feet in the direction you want to travel. The head should be kept steady and eyes fixed firmly on the ball.

The Chop

Step One:
Move alongside the ball and approach the ball with a "Side-On" position. Plant the non-kicking foot alongside the ball, with the toe pointing towards the ball.

Step Two:
Bring the kicking leg over the top of the ball with the lace of the shoe facing the outside of the ball. Chop down on the outside of the ball, using the laces only. Only slight contact is made with the outside of the ball.

Step Three:
Spin on the non-kicking foot towards the direction of the ball. The head should be kept steady and eyes fixed firmly on the ball.

Defending Introduction

Competitive soccer is quick and physical and tactics can change from game to game, from high pressure defending to man for man marking. Even the most technically gifted players have to be able to defend and handle themselves during games. No longer are fullbacks and midfield players the only ones required to defend, demands on forwards to close down opponents is also part of today's game.

Regardless of position, every player should display absolute determination and offer the strongest possible opposition when defending.

Main reasons why teams concede goals:

- Lack of pressure on the man with the ball: failing to close down forward passing and shooting angles, allowing the opponent to play with his head up.

- Lack of support for the challenging player: allowing one v one situations without good cover, playing too flat and with no depth.

- Failure to follow players: letting opponents get goal-side of their markers.

- Giving the ball away: lack of concentration, carelessness, and poor technique.

- Set plays and restarts: conceding goals from corners, free kicks, throw-in's. 40% of goals are scored from set plays.

The Block Tackle

Step One:
The Non-kicking foot should be placed alongside the ball (approximately 10" to the side). The ankle joint of the tackling foot must be firm and locked. The knees should be bent to lower the center of gravity. This will produce a compact and more powerful shape.

Step Two:
The head and upper body should be over the ball. The hands should be closed (make a fist). This will tighten the upper body.

Step Three:
Contact is made with the inside of the foot. Contact on the ball should be made through the horizontal mid-line and center of the ball. Quality tackling is as much an attitude as it is technique. Players must develop an aggressive attitude towards winning the ball.

The Slide Tackle

Step One:
Approach the ball from a "Side-On" position. Keep the head steady and eyes fixed firmly on the ball. While turning sideways into the tackle, extend the closest arm to the ball and reach for the ground. This will help take the weight off the upper body as you slide to the ground. At the same time collapse the leg closest to the ball to get to the ground quickly.

Step Two:
When on the ground alongside the ball, extend the upper leg and, using a sweeping action, attempt to win the ball.

Step Three:
If you cannot keep possession of the ball, then all attempts should be made to redirect the ball away from the opponent. The slide tackle should only be used as a last resort to dispossess a player. As you will be lying on the ground it will be a disadvantage should the tackle not be successful.

The psychological aspect of tackling plays a vital role in the outcome of any competitive soccer game. A successful tackle in the game can install confidence not only in the challenging player, but in the team as a whole. It is estimated that each player will face approximately forty individual confrontations per game. The more these individual battles are won the greater success the team has.

Tips to Consider:

- Make your first tackle count, this will give you confidence and impose authority over the player you are marking.

- Be aggressive and focus on the ball.

- Blank out any distractions and don't be intimidated by the fans.

- Don't get involved in "trash talking", this will only take away from your concentration. Don't be half hearted in the tackle. Go 100% for the ball or don't go at all.

Knowing "when and when not" to tackle is a very important quality for smart defending. Good defenders will pick the right time to win the ball, knowing that the pressure is on the attacker to beat his man. Experienced defenders will look to slow down the attacker and eliminate the momentum the attacker may have. This allows time for teammates to recover back goal side of the ball.

Tips to consider:

- Approach the attacker cautiously if he has good possession of the ball. Slow down your approach speed on your last few steps.

- Don't stop too close to the defender. This is when you are at your most vulnerable, because the exact moment you plant your feet to transfer your weight, good forwards will play the ball past you. You can compensate by stopping approximately 2 yards away from the attacker, then slowly edge in for the tackle. Watch the ball. Cunning forwards will use a variety of body and head feints to throw you off balance. Players lie, but the ball does not.

Timing a tackle is an art in itself. You must assess the flight of the ball quickly. Does your opponent have good control over the ball or is he still trying to get the ball under control? If his eyes are fixed on the ball and still trying to secure it, this is a perfect time to catch your opponent unexpectedly. Should your opponent have the ball under good control, caution is your best option.

Tips to consider:

- Watch your opponent's head. Is his head down and looking at the ball or up and scanning the field of play? If it's down, go for the ball, if it's up, be patient.

- Wait until the attacker pushes the ball out of his feet to make your tackle. This is the point where the ball is furthest away from the body and harder to control.

- The longer you delay the attack, the more time it gives your teammate to recover goal-side of the ball.

- Don't dive into the tackle if you are the last defender. Stay on your feet. Use a Slide tackle as a last resort.

Chapter 3

Coaching Methodology

The modern game of soccer has improved significantly, due to the enhanced knowledge and application in areas of tactics, fitness, nutrition and organization. Players are stronger, possess a higher level of fitness and more educated in their daily nutritional needs. Coaching is readily accepted as an important component in today's game. This was not always the case. In many countries, people involved in the game believed coaching would ruin the game and good players were born, not made.

For the past several decades, coaching organizations have slowly gained respect and proven that better teachers can produce better players. Thousands of coaches attend national coaching schools across the world to improve their knowledge of the game and in turn transfer their experiences and love of the game to train future stars.

Once a coach has acquired a certain degree of technical and tactical understanding, they then form their philosophy of the game and develop a picture of how it should be played. Some coaches prefer the Brazilian approach; others subscribe to the European methods and many coaches create a combination of both styles.

There are many common elements when it comes to coaching. Below are some of the important principles all coaches should master.

- Coaches must understand how habits are formed.
- Coaches must possess knowledge on how players learn.
- Practice sessions must be highly organized and well planned.
- Practices should progress in a logical sequence.
- Practices should be performed in relative areas of the field.

It should also be stated that "practice does not make perfect". It would be more precise to say, "practice makes permanent". This holds true for both good and bad training. The quantity of practices must never be more important than the quality of practices. Keep your sessions simple and clear.

In this chapter you will find useful information on how to organize your practice sessions more efficiently, understand the coaching formula, effective communication, how players learn and the qualities of a good coach.

Organization

Organization of the practice session is one of the most important responsibilities of the coach. It covers many aspects, from securing a field, to preparing a written plan for the practice. You should plan ahead of time and always prepare for the unexpected. Never arrive at a practice or a game without considering all the elements of organization. Players will recognize immediately when a coach is unprepared.

Good planning and thorough organization translates into confidence. If you have a well thought out plan and you are certain about how your objectives are to be achieved your players will respond appropriately.

The following are important aspects to consider when organizing your practice sessions:

Facilities

The field or practice area:

Check in advance and confirm what facilities you have for practice and make best use of those facilities. Do you have access to a full field or are you sharing a field? Search for the best playing surface if you are doing drill work or training goalkeepers. Did it rain that week? If so, do you need grids lined or the field marked? Is there shelter in case of a thunder storm? If you are using full size goals use nets. Players love seeing the ball hit the net when they score and it reduces time retrieving the ball. Portable goals are very useful for training as they can be moved around the field to suit your needs.

The area of the field:

Practice in the appropriate area of the field. For example, if you're teaching players how to pass the ball from defense, then do it in the defensive third of the field.

Equipment

Balls:

Each player should own a ball and bring
it to practice. Have players write their
name with indelible ink on the ball. Bring
extra balls in case someone forgets to
bring one. You will need a ball bag and
an inflator to keep the balls pumped up.
If you are teaching heading to young
players you may want to deflate the balls
slightly to make them softer to head.

It is also good planning to position balls on the field to reduce time
wasting. For example, when playing small-sided games have your players place a sufficient number of balls beside each goal.
This allows quick retrieval after a shot is missed and maintains the
game tempo.

Training Vests:

Training vests are needed to identify players in drills and
small-sided games. Fluorescent colors are more visible.
Remember to wash them after each practice.

Cones or Discs:

Cones or discs are important to identify boundaries in
drills and small sided-games. Without boundaries players
will navigate all over the field. The more the better, but
you should have a minimum of twelve.

The Number of players involved

Consider how many players you will have for practice. How many players do you need in each drill? Are you working in pairs or small groups? Do you have an odd or even number? If you have a player without a partner, improvise the practice to involve him or have an assistant or parent work with the player. As the coach, avoid having to team up with the odd player. You should be observing and coaching at all times.

The number of players must be appropriate to the area. It is just as big a mistake to provide too much space as it is too little. Players with poor skills need greater space.

Practice should be realistic:

Practices should reflect the game. If it doesn't happen in the game, then don't do it in your practice. Ensure that players are positioned realistically in training. For example, your goalkeeper may cheat a little in his positioning in a shooting drill because he can easily anticipate the repeated shot. Make sure he is always starting from the goal line and not creeping out too early.

Players must also perform realistically. Forwards will try harder to score goals if the defenders are working as hard to prevent them. Practice should also develop rapidly to reach a tempo that resembles game speed. If you practice slowly, you will have a slow team. If you practice explosively, you have an exciting and explosive team.

Always use full size goals (size appropriate for age group) whenever possible in practice.

Policy for injured players

Try to keep your injured players involved in the team as much possible. If they are capable of attending practice they should do so. Make sure you have seating for them, as it can be uncomfortable to stand for long periods. Can they be utilized as a temporary assistant? Have them help throw balls during drills to keep their interest up. Injured players should also sit on the team bench during games and not in the crowd to maintain a feeling of being involved.

After you have carefully planned your practice session and checked that you have all the necessary equipment, it's time to deliver your message to the players. The key to an effective practice session is simplicity and clarity. From the outset each player should understand what is expected as individuals and as a group.

The following are some key factors for you to consider when coaching in a practice session:

How to Stop and Start your practice

Players should be instructed at the beginning on how to stop and restart the practice. This is a very important point. While you are observing the practice you will want to select a "teachable moment" to stop the play. There is not a better opportunity to teach than catching the player in the act and stopping the play to correct it. Players should "freeze" instantly at the exact moment the play is halted. This will provide the coach a perfect picture to emphasize the coaching points. Once you have stopped a player to correct the mistake, walk the player through the movement, then slowly increase the movement to game speed.

How to stop the play:

Some coaches prefer to use a whistle, others their voice. If you are using a whistle let the players know that "two short blasts" of the whistle means stop. If you are using your voice, use a catchphrase such as "freeze". With young children make it into a game. See who can become the best statue when you shout freeze.

How to start the play:

After your coaching points have been addressed start the play as quickly as possible. Return a moving ball back to the player who was in possession to make the game instantly live. Simply call out "Play" to get them going.

Note: keep your stoppage time to a minimum or you will lose the tempo of the practice. Make your point and get them playing again as quickly as possible. Remember that players want to play and not stand around.

Conditioned Games

Conditioned games are commonly used.
These are usually small-sided games
that have restrictions placed upon them.
Its purpose is to isolate a specific skill or
tactic. For example, a coach may place a
condition that players may only use "one
touch" when receiving the ball.
This restriction is designed to develop
players' awareness of supporting teammates and increases the tempo of the
game.

However, you must use conditioned play selectively as it can often be
unrealistic.
Forcing a player to play "one touch" when he may not have support is
both unrealistic and impractical. Conditioned games need to reflect real
game situations and problems. They should be used occasionally and
limited to short periods and always concluded with free play.

Observation:

Analysis is based on observation. Make sure that your players are following your instructions. Always coach what you see and do not fabri-
cate situations. Support your observation with facts.

Relative areas to coach:

Coach in the relevant thirds of the field. Attacking drills should be performed with a full size goal and in the attacking third. Specific practices
for midfielders should be rehearsed in the middle third and defending in
the defensive third of the field.

Have an understanding of the topic you are teaching:

You should have an understanding of the technical and tactical elements of the topic you are teaching. Do your homework. Research
books, watch videos and talk with other coaches to help prepare your
session. The practice should move from simple to complex.

Be single minded:

You cannot teach several aspects of the game at one time. Focus on a theme such as the correct use of the push pass. Stick with it no matter how many other problems arise. Young children will not retain the information if you clutter the session with too many coaching points.

Warm Up's and Cool Down's

It is not necessary to spend time performing warm-ups with players age 9 and under. You can however implement a fun drill to capture their interest for the upcoming session. Warm ups and stretching are important for older players. Remember that you are not just preparing the body for practice but also the mind. Warms-ups traditionally tend to be repetitive. Try varying your warm-up each session, sometimes with the ball, other times without ball. Whatever you choose, keep your warm-up to a maximum of 10 minutes. Cool down older players after each practice.

After your warm up get players working as soon as possible. Try starting your session with a small sided game as opposed to always concluding the session with a game.

Selecting teams and small groups:

When selecting teams for small-sided games and group drills, do not have the players select.
Too often the same player is picked last, which leaves the player with a negative experience. Allowing players to pick teams also takes valuable time away from your practice session.

The simplest and most efficient method for selecting groups is to have all your players face you in a straight line. Move along the line and assign each player a number or a team name.

Use your imagination when making teams or small groups. Give each team a name such as the "dragons" or "super heroes" for younger players. World Cup team names can be used for older players such as "USA" versus "England".

Identify each team with colored training vests. Stay away from having one team remove their shirts (skins). Children can easily get sun burned in hot conditions and some players are very self-conscious about their body. You do not want to place any child in an embarrassing situation.

Ensure quality service

This is a very important point, which is often overlooked by coaches. The quality of the service a player receives will have a direct effect on their ability to perform the task at hand. You must teach players from the beginning how to correctly serve a ball to their teammates. Young players should know how to roll the ball at the correct speed and be able to throw the ball to a player's head, chest and thigh. A two handed throw is always more reliable. Young players have a tendency to throw with one hand.

When teaching your players to serve the ball demonstrate the following:

- Kneel on one knee when rolling the ball. This enables the player to recover the ball moe quickly should they have to retrieve it.
- Release the ball from "waist height" when the service is meant for the thigh. Players should be standing with legs positioned one in front of the other for good balance.
- Release the ball from "chest height" when the service is meant for the head. Players should be standing with legs positioned one in front of the other for good balance.

You can also have your assistant coaches and parents serve the ball when working with the novice players.

Note: Special consideration should be given when serving a ball to head for a player who is wearing glasses. Follow these simple instructions:

- First deflate the ball so it is soft to head. Allow the player to feel the ball so he knows how soft it is.
- Have the player hold the ball in both hands while bouncing the ball off the forehead.
- Take the ball and slowly demonstrate how fast you intend to serve the ball. This way they know what to expect on the first serve.
- The player's chin should be tucked in slightly to present more of the forehead to the ball. First serve should be very slow, soft and from close range.
- Gradually build up the speed of the serve and distance as the player grows in confidence.
- If the player makes a mistake and the ball hits his glasses, then start again from step two.

Step by step example of how to coach a practice session

Step One: What's the Topic?

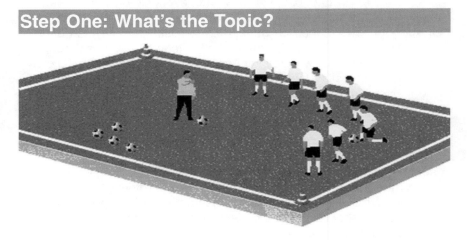

When you are ready to teach your session bring in all players and describe and demonstrate your topic. Be simple and clear. Remember when teaching "a picture tells a thousand words."
If you feel uncomfortable demonstrating have one of your better players perform the skill.

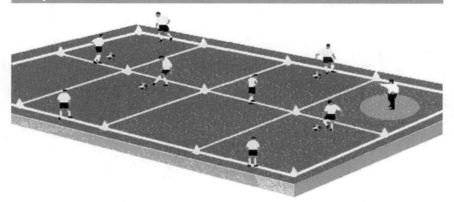

After you have made your coaching points and demonstrated, let the players practice the topic. When the players are practicing, stand outside the practice area so you can see all groups working. Observe that the practice is being carried out according to the organizational plan. Observe the general performance of the group and that all players are following your instructions. If most of the players are performing the task incorrectly it is usually because:

a. Your instructions were not clear enough.
b. Your demonstration was not clear enough.
c. The players physically are not ready to perform the task.

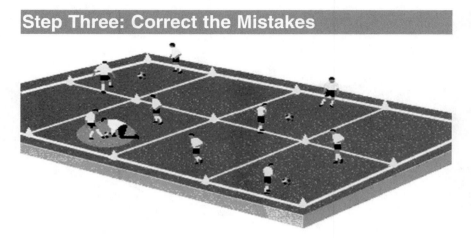

If most of the players are having problems, bring in the entire group and explain and demonstrate. If the task is too much physically for the players, improvise to an easier level. If only a few of the players are having problems, allow the other players to continue practicing while you correct the mistakes of the individuals.

When it's time to progress to the next drill, bring in all the players and explain and demonstrate what you are looking for. Be careful to progress at the correct point and not just go through a timed schedule. 50% of your practice time should be spent on quality practices to improve technique. Remember to keep your groups small, whenever possible, one ball each or one ball between two players.

Step Five: Relate the Topic to a Game

At least half of your practice time should be spent playing small or full-sided games. Emphasis should be place on applying the topic you have practiced in game related situations.

Always try to end practice on an exciting note. Too often players finish practice feeling tired and not looking forward to the next practice. Try to create an atmosphere where when you finish, players actually want to continue playing. Players will look forward to the next practice and anxious to return.

All practice sessions should have a logical sequence of progression, from simple to complex, with each stage evolving at the correct time.

One of the realities of youth coaching is that teaching time is extremely limited. Coaches often fall into the trap of wanting to do too much in one session. Do not just go through a set time schedule, by progressing from drill to drill every ten minutes or so. Players do not develop this way. Some players improve quickly, while others need more time.

Fundamentals should be your starting point whether you're teaching skills or tactics. After players understand the basic concepts and have mastered the techniques they should be challenged progressively in game like situations.

It is worth stating that team tactics are totally dependent upon the players' ability to execute the technical components of those tactics. For example, can your players pass the ball diagonally behind a defense? Can they control the ball in tight areas? Do they possess the ability to dribble past an opponent? Do they win head balls in set-plays? All of these are techniques which tactics are built upon. Remember that you cannot build a foundation on sand. The fundamentals must be strong and engrained in your players to a point of habit.

Without players who possess good technique, your time invested in team organization and principles of play will be fruitless. With players of high technical ability, the foundation will be strong to apply those techniques in skillful and tactical situations.

It is of paramount importance that coaches understand how quality technique is developed and implement a coaching regimen to challenge players to a level of technical excellence. "Practice does not make perfect". Rather, "Practice makes permanent." To reach a level of technical perfection, the technique must be isolated and performed until it becomes habit. Three important components are needed to rapidly develop good habits.

1. Repetition:

Repetition is important in developing the motor memory patterns to enable the players to execute each technique automatically, without thinking, so this becomes an ingrained habit. The practices should be designed to ensure that each player is getting as many touches on the ball as possible. Have players perform drills in small numbers. The larger the number, the less contact a player will make with the ball.

2. Consistent Quality:

Repetition can be a dangerous thing if the skill is being rehearsed incorrectly. The mechanics involved in each execution of the technique must be accurate and consistent. Aim for an 80% success rate. The coach must be the facilitator in ensuring that poor technique is detected early and precise information is provided to the player to correct the problem. The coach must know the mechanical movements involved in each technique to be able to correct those techniques.

3. Explosive Movements:

As soon as possible players must practice the technique at a speed that simulates match play. Slow practices will develop slow players and up-tempo practices will develop fast and explosive players. Never sacrifice quality for speed when practicing technique.

Step by step example of how to progress a practice session

Step One - The Basics

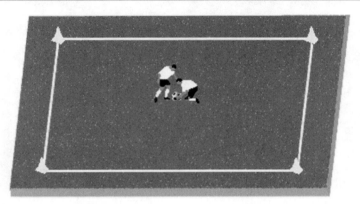

Start with the fundamentals and ensure that the player understands the basic mechanics involved in the technique. This stage should be unopposed (no defenders) and the ball should be static. Develop the practice slowly to ensure that correct habits are established from the beginning.

At this basic level of instruction you will have to get down on your knees and physically hold the player's foot to show the correct placement of the standing and kicking foot.

In this example two players are positioned in a grid 10 yards x 10 yards. One player kneels holding the ball firmly between his hands. The other player alternates stepping towards the ball and performing the mechanics of the low driven shot.

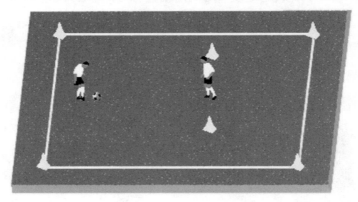

After a player demonstrates good shape when kicking a static ball, the next logical progression is to have the player hit a rolling ball. Balls can be rolling away from you, towards you, or across your body. In this example we have the ball rolling towards the player. The ball should be rolled out slowly at first, then increase the speed of the serve to challenge the player.

In this progression we have two players positioned in a grid 10 yards by 10 yards. One player is the server, the second a receiver. The server stands in between the two cones and rolls the ball towards the receiver. The receiver steps towards the ball and shoots the ball back to the server. After shooting the ball, the receiver must return to the starting position. Both players alternate roles.

The players are not trying to score goals at this stage, just repeating and reinforcing quality mechanics.

The players have now developed a feeling for striking a moving ball. Now it's time to add a little pressure, but not too much. At these early stages everything should be geared towards success and allowing the player to build confidence in the new skill. At this level you are conditioning the opposition to be passive. A defender going full speed to win the ball will not help the developing player, as he will rarely get a shot at goal.

In this example the goalkeeper is the player who is passive. He has been instructed not to go full out to stop the ball. As the drill progresses he will be encouraged to be more realistic and defend the goal like game conditions.

The players are positioned in a grid 20 yards x 40 yards. One player is placed each side of the goal and the third acts as a goalkeeper. The goalkeeper starts the practice by rolling the ball to one of the players. The player tries to score past the goalkeeper. The ball must travel between the flagpoles or cones and below head-height of the goalkeeper to count. Goals are awarded in the following manner:

- 3 goals if the player scores on first touch
- 2 goals if the player takes two touches before scoring
- 1 goal if the player takes three or more touches before scoring.

The player on the opposite side must always be alert to strike the ball when it comes into his end from a shot. If the goalkeeper saves the shot, he turns around and rolls the ball out to the opposite player. The player in goal should be rotated with the outfield players. Keep a record of the score to determine the champion. Again, the emphasis is on repetition. By playing both sides, time in retrieving the ball is minimized considerably.

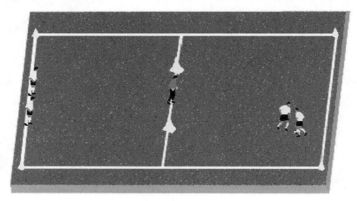

At this stage a defender is introduced. This will test the player in a more realistic scenario.

We are still working in grids and concentrating on repetition. The practice layout with players on each side of the goal minimizes time lost retrieving the ball.

In this example, five players are positioned in a grid 20 yards x 40 yards. Two players are positioned either side of the goal and the goalkeeper positioned between the flags.

The goalkeeper starts the practice by rolling the ball to one of the players. The first player to the ball tries to score past the goalkeeper, the second must defend and if they win the ball they may also shoot. The ball must travel between the cones and below head-height of the goalkeeper to count.

The practice is now conducted in a more realistic environment and in the relevant third of the field. We test the players against real defending and a goalkeeper who should be determined to win the ball.

In this stage the players are divided into pairs and placed on the end line at opposite sides of the goal. Each pair is assigned a number. The goalkeeper starts the practice by serving the ball out towards the edge of the penalty area. On distributing the ball, the goalkeeper calls out a number such as 1, 2, 3, or 4 etc. The pair selected then run out to the ball. First player to get to the ball becomes the attacker, the second acts as the defender. The defender must attempt to win the ball, and the attacker tries to score. The defender becomes the attacker if he can win possession. After a shot is taken, both players return to their starting positions.

This drill can further be developed to playing 2 v 2, 3 v 3 or 4 v 4, making each stage more game like.

The final test is always the game. Your progression should always conclude with a full match. Your coaching points during the session should be transferred into the game. Players need to see the "big picture". How does the skill fit into the team concept? Where and when should it be applied?

In this example the players are divided into two equal teams. Players are encouraged to shoot at each and every opportunity. Allow players the freedom to experiment and enjoy playing.

Communication

A coach can communicate in two ways, by showing or by speaking. The more senses involved in the learning process, the greater the chance a player will retain the information. Often new coaches are intimidated by facing a group of players, whether it's to talk or demonstrate. A coach who has not played the game may feel uncomfortable demonstrating. On the other hand, a coach with substantial playing experience may feel equally uncomfortable speaking in front of an audience. Both situations are a matter of experience and confidence.

This section will provide you with tips on how to communicate by showing and speaking.

One of the most effective forms of communication is by showing. There is an old saying "a picture tells a thousand words". On the practice field coaches are painting mental pictures for their players all the time. The more precise and clear those pictures are, the more likely it will be transferred into the game.

There are several ways coaches can visually communicate information to their players, these are:

By a Physical Demonstration:

If you are confident in your technical ability you should always show a player how it is done as opposed to telling him how it's done. When players see it, they believe it's possible.
The demonstration should be clear and of high standards. If you are uncomfortable demonstrating, select one of your most proficient players to demonstrate the skill. Demonstrating can also bring a certain degree of respect from the players, use it to your advantage.
Some coaches invite a guest professional player or a college player to their practices to demonstrate. This is a great way for younger players to watch and emulate the skills of experienced players.

By using Visual Aids:

A physical demonstration is not the only way to show players. The use of chalk boards, instructional videotapes, game videos, books, handouts and television should all be incorporated throughout the season.

Chalk boards:

Mostly used in a classroom or locker room setting. It is limited visually and often used for X's and O's sessions. Make sure you always have chalk and an eraser. Carry extra in your kit bag for away games.

Instructional Videos

There is large variety of instructional videos on the market, some good, some not so good. Talk to other coaches for recommendations. Select tapes that are age appropriate for the group you are coaching.

Game Videos

Take a camcorder and have a parent or an assistant record your games and practices. This is a perfect way for you to analyze player and team performances. You can review mistakes or feature highlights at team meetings. Use a tripod whenever possible so the finished product is steady. Focus in on players to see the action close up.

Books and Hand Outs

Recommend books for your players to buy. There are many good coaching books specifically designed for players with information on skills, nutrition and fitness.

Reinforce your practice coaching points with handouts. Highlight the key points and provide diagrams wherever applicable. Develop a manual for set plays and restarts so players know their specific roles and responsibilities. If you have a team locker room, post game responsibilities for each player on the notice board.

Television

Have a team meeting and watch a professional soccer game. Younger players should watch how professionals play. Ask each player to watch the player in his or her position.

Do it by Speaking:

Many people are intimidated by speaking in front of a crowd, but confidence can be developed if you follow a few simple rules. The most important thing is to keep it simple and clear. Preparation is key. Have an idea of what you are going to say and when you're going to say it. The following are important rules for you to use when speaking to a group of players:

Have something of value to say

Don't just talk to hear your own voice. Have something important to say or don't speak at all.

Think before you speak

Take a second or two before you respond to a question.

Be certain of the meaning of the words

Don't use words you don't understand.

Avoid jargon

Don't use words that sound too technical. Keep it short and simple. Do not waste time with lectures. If you don't know how to say it simply, don't say it at all!

Speak clearly

Don't mumble. Speak clear enough for everyone to understand you. Avoid talking too fast. If you have an accent, slow down and ensure your dialog is clear.

Vary your volume

Don't be monotone. Try to vary the volume and tempo of your speech. If you are describing an explosive movement, let your voice reflect it. If you are calming players down, speak softly.
Always talk past the most distant player. This way you will be sure that everyone can hear you.

Be positive

Keep your comments positive. Try positive reinforcement at each and very opportunity.

Watch the group while speaking

Look directly into your players' eyes when you speak. Make sure that your players are paying attention and watching you when you talk. It will help if you position them to avoid any distractions behind you.

If it's a sunny day, have the sun in your face so the direct sun light does not distract the players.

To coach effectively you must possess knowledge of how players learn. You should frequently remind yourself of what it is like to live in a child's world. Players are unique psychologically, physically and emotionally and it is important to understand and appreciate the differences between players at various age levels.

This section will provide you with pointers on how players learn and some of the character traits.

Players must have an interest

Before you can improve a player, he must have a desire and an interest to participate. As a coach you cannot force a player to be interested, he is or he isn't. Particularly with younger players, it is often the parents who made the decision to sign up for soccer. Some of these players simply do not want to be there. The best you can do, as a coach, is to make the soccer as fun and enjoyable as possible to spark the interest of the child. If the player does not respond, it may never have been meant for him to play soccer. As much as it hurts, not everyone loves soccer.

Players should be enthusiastic

Enthusiastic players want to play longer, practice harder and have an open mind when it comes to learning new ideas.

Players should see good examples

Encourage your team to watch professionals play. This is the highest level for your players to aspire to. Players need role models to emulate. Players will learn by watching and copying the skills and habits of their stars. Players also need good examples in practice. The coach must set high, yet attainable standards for the team.

Players learn through habit-forming practices

Players need to develop good habits. To achieve this, you must have three qualities in every practice. These are repetition, consistent quality and explosive movements. Repetition is vital to engraining the movement until it becomes second nature. Quality assures that the repeated movement is good and that we are not investing time reinforcing bad habits. And last, but not least, the movements must be developed as quickly as possible to a speed, which simulates match play.

Players learn by goal setting and feedback

From the first day of practice through the entire season you should set performance goals for your players and the team as a whole. These goals should be realistic and attainable. Always calculate on the side of success. When these objectives are achieved, reestablish new goals. Provide feedback to players in a positive manner and explain how they can improve upon their mistakes.

The Qualities of a good coach

Good coaches possess some fundamental qualities. It is not all about your win/loss record. Ironically, you can do a great job coaching and still not win. Conversely, you can have a successful record by just having the good fortune of better players. Regardless of the level you are coaching, the game should be a fun and a learning experience for your players.

Below are qualities of good coaching.

A good coach must:

Be enthusiastic
Enthusiasm is infectious. Regardless of how your day went, always show up to practice with enthusiasm.

Have integrity
Coach and play by the rules. Set an example of good sportsmanship after every game, regardless of the result. Be honest and upfront to players and parents.

Be a good listener
Listen to your players' problems or concerns. Encourage feedback regarding games and training sessions.

Set high standards
A good coach will always challenge his players to higher standards both on and off the field.

Be organized
If there is one controllable factor in coaching it is organization. Good coaches plan ahead and consider all aspects.

Be knowledgeable
You should have knowledge of the basic principles of the game: skills, tactics, laws, safety, management, nutrition and fitness.

Eager to learn
To continue your development you should obtain a coaching certification, attend clinics, read books, watch videos and talk with other coaches with greater experience.

Chapter 4

Team Management

Team Management deals with factors other than coaching skills and principles of the game.
It involves handling issues with players and parents such as playing time and behavioral expectations on the sidelines. It is the attention to detail in areas such as pre-game, half time and post game preparation. It encompasses a wide variety of topics, which are crucial to the harmony, and structure of the team.

In this chapter you will find management tips for practice, games, players and for evaluations.

Equipment Check List

- Prepared written practice session.
- Copies of practice session for Assistant Coaches.
- Field Inspection.
- Player Attendance Form.
- Clip Board with plastic cover.
- Stop Watch.
- Cell Phone for emergencies.
- Whistle.
- Soccer Balls.
- Practice Vests.
- Cones.
- Portable Goals/Nets.
- Water.
- Ice and Cooler.
- Medical Kit.
- Team announcements for next game/practice.
- Coaches Kit Bag, Rain Gear, Towel, Inflator and Pin.

Pre- Game

Before the game starts you should consider the following:

Equipment needs for the game and warm up

For the game
- Uniforms (what color? home or away?)
- Game Balls (4 recommended)
- Pump and Inflator
- Corner Flags (6)
- Goal Nets
- First Aid Kit
- Medical Release Forms
- Cell Phone
- Player Passes
- Ice and Cooler
- Water

For the warm up
- Warm up "T" shirts
- Balls
- Cones
- Training Vests

Field Inspection
- Make sure field markings are visible.
- Check goal nets
- Select best suited footwear for the playing conditions.
  Screw-ins for wet surfaces, molded soles for dry conditions.

Find your Half Time Location
- Find out before the game where you will regroup at half time.
- Look for a shaded area in hot conditions.
- Look for shelter on wet days.

Check on Injured Players
- Before you can select a team line up you may have to check
  on the injury status.

Decide on a line-up - Submit Team Roster
- Time to decide on your team line up. Some leagues may
  require that you submit a team roster or show player ID's
  before the game commences.

Pre-game team talk

- Keep the pre-game team talk brief and to the point. Identify a few main goals for the team to accomplish. You can be specific to each player in the minutes leading up to the game.

Warm up

- Allow 25 to 30 minutes for a team and goalkeeper warm up.
- Younger players under 10 may only need about 10 minutes.

Greet Officials

- Greet the officials before the game. It's a good way to get to know them on a personal level.

Coin Toss

- Captain to decide which side to select. Always take the advantage in the first half. For example, play with the wind in the first half, it may die down in the second half.

Half Time

At the interval you should consider the following:

Meet at your half time location

- Look for a shaded area in hot conditions.
- Look for shelter on wet days.

Rest

- Have your players sit down on the ground and relax.
- You are allowed a maximum of 15 minutes rest period in eleven-a-side games. Sometimes the referee may ask for 10 minutes.
- Take the full 15 minutes if your players are tired, you have only a few substitutes or if the weather is hot.
- Agree to 10 if minutes the weather is cold or conditions are deteriorating.

Fluids

- Players should have a small drink of water. Avoid drinking too much.
- Have drinks ready in paper cups or bottles to save time.

150

Check Injuries

- Check for any new injuries or recurring injuries to your players. Get treatment if necessary.

Review first half performance

- Because of the short time, limit your talk to 3 to 4 points.
- Be specific and clear.
- Make appropriate adjustments tactically based on your first half observations. Refer to your notes and confer with your assistant coaches.

Warm Up

- Use two minutes of your half time break for a quick stretch.

Post Game

At the conclusion of the game you should consider the following:

Shake hands with opposing team and officials

- At the end of the game, players and coaches usually line up facing each other on the halfway line, walk past each other and touch hands and say "good game". Coaches are usually last in line and shake hands.
- Always be a sportsman regardless of the result.
- It is also a nice gesture and sets a good example for the coach to seek out the referee and assistant referees and thank them.

Fluids

- Players should have a drink of water to replenish fluid lost during the game.
- Have drinks ready in paper cups or bottles to save time.
- Parents usually take turns providing refreshments after games.

Check Injuries

- Check for any new injuries or recurring injuries to your players. Get treatment if necessary.

Cool Down

- Players should perform a brief 5-minute cool down after each game.
- Keep this a routine, even when you lose.

Review game briefly

- Review the game very briefly and only emphasize the positives. Your next practice session is the place to be detailed and comprehensive. Sometimes after a loss, frustration can rule. It is good policy to restrain your comments until you have had an opportunity to reflect on the game.

Team announcements

- Make appropriate announcements for your next practice or game to parents and players.

Collect and check equipment

- Make sure all the equipment is collected and accounted for.
- Have the team captain and several players be responsible for this duty.

Replenishment

- Thirty minutes after any competition suggest your players eat a meal high in complex carbohydrates to help restore the body's blood sugar (glycogen levels).

Players' Responsibilities

Hand to your players at first team meeting.

Ready to Play
Players should bring the following with them to every training session:

- Inflated ball.
- Your own cool water (cool water is absorbed faster).
- Shin guards.
- Soccer shoes and indoor shoes (be prepared for the weather).
- Tape.
- Extra shoe laces.
- Emergency phone #'s.
- A complete change of clothes (especially socks).
- Keepers bring gloves, shirt and long pants in case the field is poor.

In short, you should be ready for anything! Put these items in your bag the night before your session so that you do not have to hunt them down and thus be late for training the next morning! Be at practice 10 - 15 minutes early, in time to get your gear on so that you are ready to start on time.

Practicing on your own

The best thing that you can do is get your friends together, set up a field, choose sides and play. Sometimes, invite players that are older than you, and better. The most important thing is that you play, whether it is 1 v 1, 2 v 2, 4 v 4, or even 2 v 3. It doesn't matter, just play. If you can not get others to join you, spend as much time with the ball as you can. Find a wall to kick against, invent juggling games for yourself, try to chip a ball into a garbage can from various distances, be creative, have fun. You have to claim responsibility for your own development. Once you realize how much fun it is to play the game with skill, you may never want to stop!

Selecting a Team Captain

Careful consideration should apply when selecting your team captain. Some coaches allow the players to vote for their captain. However, this can become a popularity contest and sometimes result in the wrong player being selected. The captain is an extension of the coaching staff and should serve as a "go between" for the players. On occasion players feel a little uneasy talking directly to the coach, so relaying their concerns through the team captain is an alternative.

The captain should have several attributes. Below is a checklist of the qualities you should look for in a team captain:

A team captain must:

- Be a leader on and off the field.
- Be a starter on the team.
- Be positive and encouraging to teammates.
- Be vocal.
- Be respected.
- Be honest.
- Be a good sportsman.
- Be level headed and not get into fights on the field.
- Be reliable.
- Be loyal.

Once you have made your choice of team captain, an individual meeting should be arranged. During the meeting you should explain the roles and responsibilities of being the captain.

Here are some assignments for your team captain:

- Take the team for warm ups during practice and pre-game.
- Greet game officials.
- Coin toss
- Select sides for kick off.
- Hold informal team meetings.
- Help collect equipment at end of practice.

Sample skill stations used for try-out evaluations

Evaluation Stations

Use these stations to assist you in objectively evaluating your players. This is a good format for assessing players as part of your try out procedure.

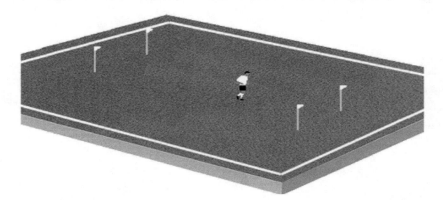

Line up and run 40 yards. Record total time.

Equipment:
Stopwatch, 2 cones.

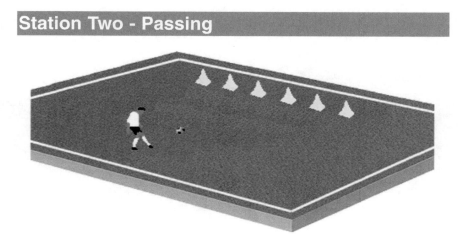

Pass three balls accurately using the "push pass", with each foot.
Aim for the middle slot. Indicate slots hit (10pts,5pts,1pt).
Middle slot = 10 points, next to middle slots = 5 points, end slots = 1
point.

Equipment:
6 balls, 6 cones.
Adjust passing distance from cones to make appropriate for age group.

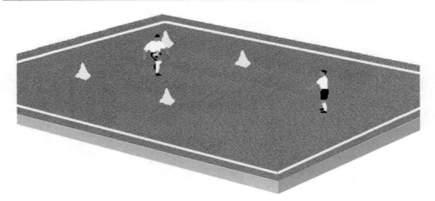

Serve 6 high lofted throws for player to control with head, chest, thighs or feet. Ball must not drop within the square before controlling. Award (10pts) for each successful attempt.

Equipment:
4 cones, 6 balls.

Dribble from the staring cone, weave through slalom course and back to starting cone.
Record total time.

Equipment:
6 cones, 1 ball.
Stop Watch.

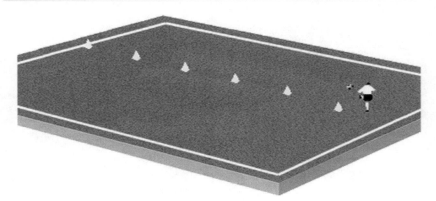

Using the lofted pass (aerial), kick 3 balls for distance with each foot.
Cones are placed at 10-yard intervals.
Record length of kicks for each foot.

Equipment:

6 cones, 6 balls.

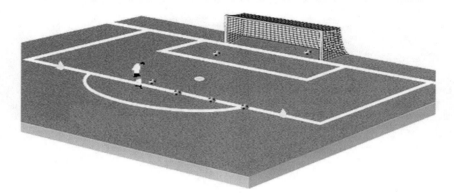

Shoot 6 balls into an undefended goal.
Record number of goals scored.

Equipment:
6 balls.

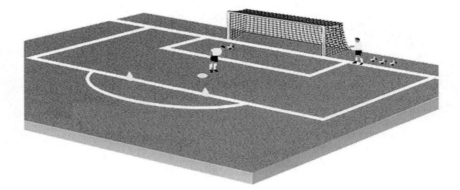

Head 6 balls served at head height into an undefended goal.
Record number of goals scored.

Equipment:
6 balls.

Chapter 5

Equipment

It is important to consider your entire equipment requirements before the season commences. This chapter provides you with a thorough guide to your equipment needs and advice on each item.

Uniforms

There are a variety of companies supplying game uniforms and accessories. They differ in quality, range and price. Find a kit that fits your budget. When selecting a uniform ensure that it is lightweight, breathable, practical and attractive to your players.

Soccer shoes should be supple, preferably leather, have a snug fit and cared for after each game. A young player's foot size will change each season, so common sense should be used in purchasing new shoes. Older players who are serious about the game should have two pairs of soccer shoes. One pair with molded soles for hard playing conditions and another with screw in studs for wet surfaces.

Balls

Ideally you should have one ball per player, or at a minimum, one ball between two players. Invest in buying hand-stitched balls. Plastic or molded balls can cause poor habits and are often uncomfortable to head or control.

Select the right size ball for the appropriate age group.

Ages 5 to 8 - Size 3 ball
Ages 9 to 12 - Size 4 ball
Ages 13 and over - Size 5 ball

Always remember to take a pin and inflator to each game and practice.

Cones

You need to have a good supply of cones to mark off boundaries for your practice grids and small-sided games. Minimum 24 cones.

Training Vests

Bibs are necessary to identify teams in small-sided games and individual players in drills such as forwards and defenders. Go for florescent colors like yellow or green. Minimum 12 bibs.

Nets

Whenever possible use nets on the goals. There is nothing more exciting for a player than watching the ball hit the back of the net.

Corner Flags

Corner flags are ideal for making goals in small-sided scrimmages. They also provide a better visual target for the players.

First Aid Kit

You should always have a well-stocked First Aid kit at every practice and game. Routinely check to make sure you have all the necessary supplies in your kit. Also keep emergency telephone numbers, directions to local hospital and change for a pay phone in the kit.
What you need in your Kit
- Latex gloves
- Band-Aids
- Adhesive tape
- Gauze pads
- Scissors
- Tweezers
- Ice pack
- Antiseptic
- Alcohol pads
- Sun Screen
- Thermometer
- Ace bandage
- Sting relief
- Mirror
- Tissues
- Medical release forms

Cellular Phone

If possible take a cellular telephone along with you to practice in case of emergencies. If you don't have a cellular phone make sure you have change for a pay phone. Tape a quarter and a map showing the most direct route to the closest hospital to the inside of your Medical Kit. Always have emergency contact numbers for each player at every practice and game.

Ice

Always take a cooler with plenty of ice. Put some zip lock bags in the cooler for ice bags.

Water

Ensure each player brings a bottle of water to every practice and game. Allow players appropriate water breaks, especially in hot conditions. Have each player write his name with an indelible pen on his water bottle. Don't allow players to drink from the same bottle.

Coaching Grids

Use grids to mark off boundaries for practices and small-sided games.

Coaching Attire

Coaches should dress appropriately for practice sessions and games. Presenting a professional image for your players is very important. Do not coach in street clothes. This sets a bad example for your team. Wear a shirt, shorts, socks and select the correct footwear for the field conditions.
Other items to include in your coaching bag are:
- Sweat Suit.
- Rain Gear.
- Towel.
- Whistle.
- Clipboard.
- Stop Watch.
- Notebook.
- Sun Screen

Soccer Made Easy Software

The most complete coaching program world wide

Soccer Made Easy are the leaders in the production and development of multimedia coaching content. Thousands of clubs, coaches and players in over 80 countries have adopted Soccer Made Easy software as their primary coaching tool.

The "World Youth Training Program" is also available in CD-ROM. Unlike videocassettes or books, the software program provides you with hundreds of printable topics you can take right to practice. The unique animation sets it apart from other products by using practice sessions that are fully animated, it's like watching your own soccer clinics right at home. No need to take notes or draw diagrams, it's all done for you. We are confident that Soccer Made Easy coaching software will become a useful part in your coaching preparation. But you'll never know how useful it can be until you try it.

To view all of the Soccer Made Easy coaching CD-ROM's go to www.soccerclinics.com or www.reedswain.com

SoccerClinics.com
your link to online coaching

Also Available from Reedswain

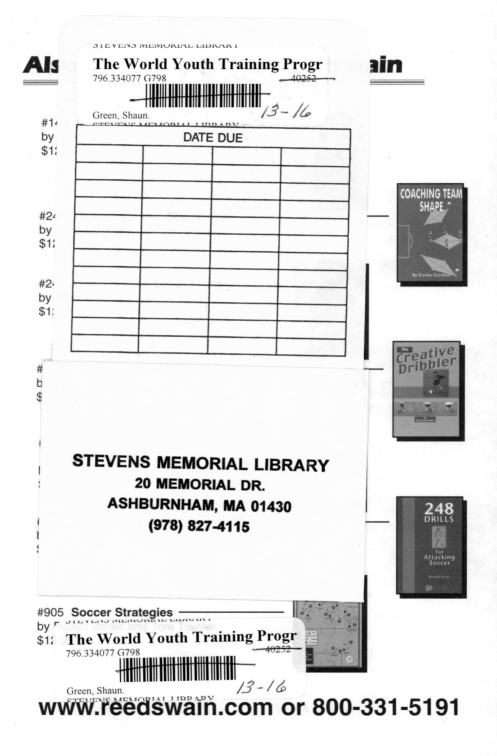